The Complete Classroom

Steven Hastings is one of the UK's leading education journalists. He has been a regular contributor to the TES since 1997, and his work has dealt with almost every aspect of contemporary school life. He has been writing for the weekly series *The Issue* since its inception in 2002.

The **TES** is the UK's leading publication covering primary, secondary and further education; it is also the market leader for teaching job vacancies. It is published every Friday and is available from newsagents or on subscription (tel: 01858 438805 or via www.tes.co.uk).

Want to be up to date on educational thinking, but never have the time to read all of the books? *The Complete Classroom: Issues and Solutions for Teachers* offers a comprehensive overview of the challenges and concerns facing modern schools. Everything from tackling truancy to teaching children to write, from teenage suicide to pets in the classroom, this easy-to-digest guide cuts through the jargon to offer professional advice, expert opinion and practical ideas for better teaching.

Divided into three themed sections, the book provides a comprehensive and accessible introduction to the main issues affecting contemporary schools:

- The healthy classroom, including dealing with junk food and bereavement.
- The thinking classroom, from emotional intelligence to personalized learning.
- The well-rounded classroom, covering everything from going green to pupil power.

Based on the acclaimed series *The Issue* in the *Times Educational Supplement*, the book brings together Steven Hastings's vast experience and gives vital information on twenty-four key issues for teachers today. Both informative and practical, the book provides a coherent synthesis of the current key topics in teaching, illustrates each topic with first hand case studies, provides follow-up resources and shows how each topic interrelates.

Whether you're an NQT or an experienced classroom teacher, a governor or a school manager, this is the essential guide to life in schools today.

The Complete Classroom

Issues and solutions for teachers

Steven Hastings

LONDON AND NEW YORK

First published 2006
by Routledge
2 Park Square, Milton Park, Abingdon, Oxon OX14 4RN

Simultaneously published in the USA and Canada
by Routledge
605 Third Avenue, New York, NY 10017

Routledge is an imprint of the Taylor & Francis Group, an informa business

© 2006 Steven Hastings

Typeset in Goudy by
Newgen Imaging Systems (P) Ltd, Chennai, India

All rights reserved. No part of this book may be reprinted or
reproduced or utilised in any form or by any electronic,
mechanical, or other means, now known or hereafter
invented, including photocopying and recording, or in any
information storage or retrieval system, without permission in
writing from the publishers.

Notice:
Product or corporate names may be trademarks or
registered trademarks, and are used only for identification
and explanation without intent to infringe.

British Library Cataloguing in Publication Data
A catalogue record for this book is available
from the British Library

Library of Congress Cataloging in Publication Data
Hastings, Steven, 1970–
    The complete classroom : issues and solutions for teachers/
  Steven Hastings
      p. cm.
     1. Effective teaching–Great Britain. 2. Teachers–Training of–
  Great Britain. I. Title.

LB2838.H335 2006
371.100941–dc22   2005030909

ISBN13: 978–0–415–39261–7 (hbk)
ISBN13: 978–0–415–39262–4 (pbk)
ISBN13: 978–0–203–96982–3 (ebk)

Contents

Acknowledgements	vii
Introduction	viii

PART I
The healthy classroom — 1

1	The teaching voice	3
2	Truancy	10
3	Nits	17
4	Bereavement	21
5	Junk food	27
6	Homophobia	35
7	Self harm	40
8	Teenage suicide	46
9	When you're sick	52
10	Teacher's sabbaticals	58

PART II
The thinking classroom — 65

11	Using questions	67
12	Handwriting	73

13	Emotional intelligence	81
14	Thinking skills	86
15	Personalized learning	90
16	Teaching children to read	95
17	Promoting creativity	101

PART III
The well-rounded classroom — **107**

18	Going green	109
19	Using volunteers	117
20	Artists in residence	125
21	The learning environment	132
22	School links	138
23	Classroom pets	146
24	Pupil power	153

| *Resources* | 160 |
| *Index* | 173 |

Acknowledgements

Everyone at *TES Friday* magazine, where these pieces first appeared, in particular, Jill Craven, whose keen sense of the issues which matter in schools is reflected in the subjects covered.

All those who contributed to the case studies, including Roger Sharpe, Jim Goodall, Gillian Dalby, whose first-hand accounts are used here with their permission.

And special thanks to Jacqueline Yallop – author of the chapters *Junk Food* and *Artists in Residence*, reproduced here with her permission – for her invaluable help in bringing the book together.

Introduction

There are plenty of in-depth volumes for teachers wanting specialist information. Whole books are given over to the nuances of classroom body language or the intricate mysteries of job applications. This is not one of those books.

As a teacher, I always wanted to keep up to date with the most recent and important issues affecting my profession. But I didn't have the time or the energy to read 500 pages of academic study. What I wanted was a digest of the latest thinking, written in an accessible way and presented in a format I could dip into during those precious spare moments before bed. This, I hope, is that book.

The Complete Classroom brings together issues that most teachers will face at some point in their career in the classroom. Not everything is here – how could it be? – but I have tried to include a broad range of subjects. Some are inevitably more relevant for teachers at primary or secondary level, but many can be used in a variety of classrooms. Some issues – such as bereavement or pupil power – tackle subjects that are sensitive or controversial. Some offer a bite size introduction to pedagogical issues like learning styles and thinking skills. Others – like nits or artists in residence – reflect the infinite variety of classroom life.

Most of the chapters in the book first appeared in the *Times Educational Supplement* as part of a weekly series called 'The Issue'. For this volume they have been distilled and updated. Because the pieces started life in a newspaper the emphasis was on making sometimes difficult subject matter accessible and maintaining a readable style. Whilst re-working the material for this book, I've tried to keep that original spirit in mind.

Each chapter provides an overview of a particular issue. It should bring you up to speed with current practice, whilst offering some practical suggestions for your own teaching. In some cases, it may tell you all want – or need – to know. Other issues, however, may be of particular relevance in your classroom, or of special interest to you personally. With this in mind, each chapter is complemented, at the back of the book, by a list of resources and suggestions for further reading. In addition, some of the chapters are accompanied by real-life accounts, showing how teachers or schools have dealt with the issues in practice.

The book is organized in three parts. The first, 'The Healthy Classroom', explores some of the issues surrounding the well-being of both learners and teachers. The second, 'The Thinking Classroom', tries to unravel recent government initiatives and assess how current catchphrases such as 'personalized learning' translate into better teaching. The 'Well-Rounded Classroom' completes the book with a look at more diverse, even offbeat, subjects.

But if there is one thing that comes out of the many conversations with teachers that contributed to the making of this book, it is that successful education in the twenty-first century demands a holistic approach. It is not intended that each section or chapter be considered as separate from others, rather that together they should offer a series of stepping stones towards a supportive and inspiring classroom.

Part I

The healthy classroom

Children learn best when they feel well. You teach best when you feel well. It's not just a question of physical health, of course, but also of emotional well-being. In conversation with teachers, however, it becomes apparent that many children arrive in the classroom unfit to learn. And many teachers struggle through the long terms, never quite feeling at the top of their game.

It's not easy to make generalizations about what keeps people healthy and positive. All your pupils will have individual needs. Each one will be facing different challenges and demands in their life, both at school and at home. Often it is the teacher who is in the front line, having to react quickly and sensitively to a wide range of problems. There was a time when teachers would have argued that this kind of thing was not their concern. Now most of us realise that having a healthy, happy classroom is in everyone's interest.

Some of the subjects touched on here, like teenage suicide, are rare events. Others, like truancy, are all too common. And others, like self harm, may be more common than many schools realise or are willing to admit. What links them together, is that no matter how often these issues might arise, you need to be able to respond with the right advice at the right time.

But this section is not just about looking after other people. Your own needs are important. Teaching is a demanding profession and it's sometimes the things you don't think of that can make a difference. A simple measure like taking good care of your voice, for example, can help you become a more effective teacher. It may even prolong your career. Being a healthy teacher is not just about never having a day off sick – it's about being able to function to the best of your ability. With this in mind, the section closes with a look at teaching sabbaticals. It's not wrong to want to take a break. Many teachers find a change in environment revitalizes their practice, refreshes them physically and mentally and helps them recapture their enthusiasm.

Chapter 1

The teaching voice

The voice is a fundamental tool of the teaching trade. It is used to communicate information, hold attention and keep order. Teachers talk for around 60 per cent of their working day, so it's not surprising that voice problems are common. For most, that means the occasional sore throat after a particularly hard day in the classroom but, for some, it means serious damage to the vocal cords that can threaten a career. Learning to use your voice more effectively will help keep it healthy – and could make you a better teacher.

Statistics that speak loud and clear

Two separate surveys of UK voice clinics, both carried out since 2000, found that at least one in nine patients was a teacher; in Scotland, the figure was one in five. According to Voice Care Network UK, which conducted one of the studies, teachers are eight times more likely to suffer from voice problems than other professions. Other research published in the *Journal of Voice* in 1998 found that a fifth of all teachers experienced a problem with their voice during the teaching year. Another study reported in the same issue found that the same proportion of teachers, 20 per cent, had taken time off because of voice problems at some point in their career, compared with just 4 per cent of non-teachers.

Tool of the trade

Some teachers shout a lot, most teachers talk a lot, and all teachers face situations where they have to make themselves heard above background noise. Using your voice all day needn't be a problem, as long as you are using it correctly. But whereas actors at drama school will work on their voice every day, a teacher at training college will be lucky to get a morning's lecture on the subject – and if you qualified more than five years ago you may not have received any instruction at all. Not surprisingly, many teachers find that their voice is unable to cope with the demands. Research by Dr Stephanie Martin at Greenwich University in 2003, assessed the voices of 50 NQTs before they went out into the classroom. It found that 46 per cent had vocal qualities that gave cause for 'some concern', while not one was starting their teaching career with a voice of 'professional user quality'. Not surprisingly, half of the sample group lost their voice at some point during their first year in the classroom.

Pitfalls of the profession

Another factor which can put your voice at risk is stress. Physical tension in the body has a negative impact on the quality of your voice and often leads to soreness. The classic confrontational posture – with the jaw jutting forward – is a trademark of many teachers, and is particularly bad for the voice. Other problems reported by speech therapists include teachers talking in too low a register to try to sound authoritative – and even a primary teacher who talked through a fixed smile all day because she wanted to seem friendly.

All teachers need to look after their voices, but primary teachers face a particular challenge because the noise above which they need to be heard is usually at a higher pitch. Also at risk are physical education (PE) teachers who have to contend with echoing sports halls and windy playing fields.

Breathe easy

The first step to improving your use of your voice is to understand how it works. Speech is produced when breath passes over your vocal cords, causing them to vibrate. The sound is amplified by the resonating cavities in your chest, mouth and head. Then your lips, teeth and tongue shape the sound into recognizable words. It's a natural, instinctive process. So what can go wrong?

One common failing is poor breathing. Snatching shallow breaths into your mouth or chest is a common side effect of a hectic lifestyle, but doing this involves the weak muscles around your neck rather than the strong muscles in the abdomen, and this puts pressure on your vocal cords. Correct breathing, using your diaphragm, takes the pressure off your neck and shoulders, and gives power to the voice. It's important, too, that the air has a clear passage from the lungs to the larynx, which is where good posture is important. A slumped spine, hunched shoulders or a pushed-out neck could all cause tension and block the flow of air. A gentle massage of the neck and shoulders from time to time will help to relax muscles, but the way we breathe and stand are ingrained habits and it may take time and patience to change things.

Don't put up...

Serious problems with your voice don't come out of the blue. They are usually the result of prolonged misuse over weeks, months or years. And your body will provide you with plenty of warning signs along the way, if you're prepared to take note. The classic distress signals are hoarseness and sore throats, especially first thing in the morning, or a feeling that the voice is 'scratchy' and taking a long time to warm up. Perhaps you notice that your voice is getting stuck in a particular register, with less range than usual. Listen out, too, for any involuntary swoops or squeaks. If you sound like a teenager with a breaking voice, it may be because your voice is breaking in an altogether less happy sense.

...shut up!

It's easy to assume that a sore throat is just part of the job and carry on regardless, but in doing so you could be risking more serious damage. If you're struggling, take time off. An athlete who pulls a hamstring simply has to be patient, and it's the same for teachers with a sore voice. If you can't bring yourself to stay at home, you may find that a class responds charitably if you explain the problem. Set them some work and practise a little amateur sign language. At the very least, try to build some quiet lessons into your timetable, and avoid unnecessary chatter in the staffroom. And when you do find yourself having to speak, ensure that you make an extra effort to talk properly, with good breathing. Whispering may seem like a good idea but it's actually likely to make things worse because you're talking without proper breath support. If a few days' rest doesn't help, or if the problem recurs frequently, visit your GP, who will probably refer you to an ear, nose and throat specialist. If problems are dealt with in the early stages, changing a few habits should be enough to restore your voice to full health.

However, prolonged abuse of the vocal cords can lead to nodules – growths on the cords – which may require surgery.

Healthy hints

As with looking after other parts of your body, there are general do's and don'ts when it comes to voice care. For example, eating spicy foods late at night can cause a condition known as acid reflux, which damages the vocal cords. And eating too many dairy products can increase the amount of saliva you produce, bad for your voice, and not good either for those at the front of the class. Be careful, too, that you don't make a nervous habit of clearing your throat. This makes the vocal cords clash together and causes wear and tear over time. And just as a sportsman takes time to warm up his muscles before serious action, try to get in the habit of warming up your vocal cords in the morning with some gentle humming or a sing-song in the shower.

Most teachers do much less talking in the holidays, so at the start of a new term, it's important to be extra careful, and try to ease yourself into the swing of things. Finally, remember that being in good general health will strengthen your voice. Being unfit and often out of breath will affect your voice, as will any viral throat infections you pick up.

Acoustics and aspidistras

Voice problems sometimes have their roots in the room where you teach. A cavernous, echoing classroom is likely to have you pushing your voice. There may be nothing you can do, but think about how you organize the room. Is it possible, for example, to set the desks up in such a way as to bring your audience closer? Central heating is another potential source of problems. The voice works best in a moist, well-ventilated room, but many modern classrooms are hot, dry and stuffy. Most people are more sensitive to temperature than moisture; we know if a room is too hot or too cold, but can't always tell if it's too dry. But it's possible to buy gadgets that measure moisture and it may be worth persuading your school to invest in one. A good way of increasing moisture in a room is to have a few leafy plants dotted around. Opening a window will also help beat dehydration, as will having a glass of water to hand. Keeping the voice well watered is important; and most experts recommend drinking a couple of litres a day. Water at room temperature is best, and regular sipping is better than downing a large glass twice a day. Be aware that caffeine has a dehydrating effect, so too many cups of coffee won't do your voice any favours.

Speaking up for yourself

Voice care is an important health and safety issue. Every year a small number of teachers are forced out of the profession because of permanent damage to their voice. The teaching unions claim voice problems are a 'foreseeable risk' and that employers have a duty to take 'reasonable care'. So if, for example, you find yourself teaching in a classroom next to the school canteen and constantly having to make yourself heard above the noise, don't be afraid to raise your concerns. If you can't talk, you can't work – so it's in your school's interest to take the issue seriously.

In February 2002, a report published by the General Teaching Council for Scotland, *Voice and the Teaching Profession*, recommended that schools make more use of voice specialists to deliver in-service training days and advice to individuals. But the Voice Care Network warns that many UK schools are still unwilling to allocate sufficient time or money to voice training. Schools that do take the plunge are rarely disappointed. King Henry VIII school in Coventry, for example, booked a day's workshop for all its staff, and followed up with another day for those who wanted it. 'The initial idea came from the staff,' says director of studies Roger Howes, 'and everyone got a lot out of it. But I can see that this is probably the sort of thing we need to have every year or so, not just as a one-off.'

Finding your voice

Keeping your voice in good working order may seem more like a matter of personal health, rather than a classroom skill. But looking after your voice is the first step to making best use of it. Teachers want to be listened to, and having an interesting voice is almost as important as having interesting things to say. The way you use your voice will affect everything from how classes behave to how much they remember of what you tell them. It's easy to fall into the trap of sounding like a caricature of a teacher, adopting the safe, dull voice of an authority figure. Or to think that talking loudly is the key to holding attention, even though most children switch off if they feel they are being 'talked at' rather than 'talked to'.

According to Lesley Hendy, a former lecturer in drama and education at Cambridge University and now a freelance voice tutor, the most common request by teachers at her workshops is 'to learn how to shout'. But the real skill of vocal delivery is modulating pause, pace, pitch and power, which means having a voice which is in good working order, and being in control of the basics, such as breathing and posture.

Most teachers find that a relaxed, well-produced voice has more 'colour' than one that is pushed or strained, and so holds the attention of the class more easily. And while it is quite possible to learn to project the voice, it's also true that clear articulation is sometimes more important than volume when it comes to being heard clearly and easily.

Discovering the full potential of your voice can be a lifetime's journey, but even a few simple vocal exercises every day can soon bring about noticeable improvements. There are a growing number of voice books on the market, though most experts insist there's no substitute for personal instruction – at least to get you started.

In practice

As a teacher, my voice is my main weapon, and it's in constant use. I probably talk for around five hours a day, every day, but if I have a parents' evening, it can be nearer to eight hours.

I've been in teaching for over 20 years, but it was only 5 or 6 years ago that I started having problems. I'm asthmatic, which probably doesn't help, and classrooms aren't as quiet as they used to be, so you're raising your voice a lot of the time. On one occasion I lost my voice so badly that I had to pass a note to the doctor to explain what was wrong with me. I literally couldn't say a word. The doctor just shook his head and said 'Singers, actors and teachers; it's always the same'.

I realized I needed to do something to save my voice, so I asked my headteacher about the possibility of some kind of microphone. Now I wear a headset, rather like the ones pop stars use, and speak into the mouthpiece in a normal voice. My voice is amplified through speakers that can be positioned wherever I want in the classroom.

It's strange for a while, but then you forget you're using it. There's a novelty factor for the pupils too, though again, they soon get used to it. The only problem was that a colleague got the same system at the same time, and until we got our frequencies sorted out, my voice kept coming through in her room and vice versa. Very confusing for everybody.

I started off using the system every day, but now my voice has recovered I rarely need it. In any case, since I started having voice trouble I've adjusted my teaching style and I don't talk as much as I used to. I try to plan my lessons so there is some time for pupils to get on by themselves.

Most schools would benefit from a couple of microphones that can be shared when staff have problems. They cost a few hundred pounds: if someone is off sick because of vocal problems, the cost of supply will far outstrip that. It's not a case of having one day off if you lose your voice; it's taken me two to three weeks to recover.

The long autumn term is definitely the worst time. Lots of colleagues are coughing, croaking or hoarse. You get people apologising in the staffroom for not being able to have a chat. And a serious problem, like nodules on the vocal cords, can threaten a whole career. The room where I teach has good acoustics, but when I cover lessons around the school I find some classrooms more difficult. If there's any kind of echo you end up raising your voice to compete.

I look after my voice much more now. My consultant taught me the importance of keeping my voice hydrated. Every evening I hold my head over a bowl of steam and inhale – you can feel the soothing effect on your vocal cords – and I'm never without a bottle of water in school.

But why had I never been told this before? There's definitely a case for proper voice training for all teachers at college. I'm a county secretary for the National Association of Schoolmasters Union of Women Teachers (NASUWT) and, from a union perspective, schools are in breach of their duty of care if they don't make sure employees know how to use their voice safely and effectively.

Jim Goodall teaches chemistry at Abersychan comprehensive school in Torfaen, Wales.

Chapter 2
Truancy

Mitching it. Wagging it. Dogging it. Twagging it. If proof were needed that truancy is ingrained in our culture, look no further than the range of slang phrases used to describe it. Children have been bunking off and skipping lessons since the first schools were established. But the fight against truancy has never had a higher profile: sweeps by police and welfare officers, hi-tech registration systems, prison sentences and increased fines to parents of persistent non-attenders. But despite all these measures, more than eight million schooldays are lost to truancy annually, with a hardcore 2 per cent of pupils missing more than five weeks every year. And there's little sign of that figure falling.

What sort of numbers are we talking about?

Opinions vary widely, although experts agree that the Government figure of 50,000 each day is well short of the mark. One problem is the lack of consistency between schools when it comes to registering attendance.

Truancy is usually defined as 'unauthorised absence' – a phrase open to interpretation. Some Local Education Authorities (LEAs) class exclusion from school as an invalid reason for non-attendance, and so mark excluded pupils down as truants, despite Department for Education and Skills (DfES) guidelines to the contrary. Some count children who are home-educated; those convalescing from serious illness or those who leave school at lunchtime without permission, even though they do not miss any lessons. Some run truancy sweeps at a time when those who are just late are likely to be caught up in them. In contrast, while LEAs are keen to be seen to be catching truants, heads are under pressure to improve attendance rates: so some schools will mark all absences as 'authorized', providing the child brings a parental note on his or her return to school.

Nor do the figures include those pupils who register at 8.55am before disappearing again. Or those who skip the odd lesson because they don't like Mr Smith or because they owe Miss Jones some homework. And finally, there are thousands of children under 16 years of age who just don't appear on any school roll. Sometimes they are the children of illegal immigrants or Travellers. But often they have just been lost in the system. For example, a Trade Union Congress (TUC)/Mori poll in 2001 found that 100,000 children under 16 truant every day so they can hold down jobs, often using false identities.

Does truancy matter?

'Playing truant' implies that skipping school is a game. The facts tell a more disturbing story. A 1998 study found that only 8 per cent of regular truants achieved five GCSEs at A–C, while one in three failed to achieve any passes. Evidence also suggests truants have an increased likelihood of ending up homeless, unemployed and in dysfunctional relationships. Schools suffer, too. Many teachers say having a large number of irregular attenders in a class affects the progress of those who do attend regularly.

Truancy is also a waste of resources beyond the school gates. A 2005 survey of truancy sweeps by 120 LEAs in England and Wales found that they used up over 16,000 hours of police time – the equivalent of ten full-time officers – even though on an average fewer than half the children stopped were truants and four LEAs reported finding no truants at all during a combined total of 22.5 police hours.

But the most compelling argument as to why non-attendance matters – to individuals and to society at large – lies in the link between truancy and crime. Five per cent of all crimes are carried out by truants during school hours; 23 per cent of young people sentenced in court have a history of truancy; truants are three times more likely to offend than non-truants; a truancy sweep in east London led to a 70 per cent fall in car crime; almost 80 per cent of boys who truant once a week commit criminal offences. The list goes on.

Is it a growing problem?

The fight against truancy has been running for more than a century. As long ago as 1870 the authorities were concerned by non-attendance, and by the early 1900s many schools had attendance officers to round up those who weren't in class. 'What a business it was,' remarks one officer writing his memoirs in 1913, 'to get the children into the schools.'

But the problem has continued to get worse. The fact that children are maturing increasingly early means truancy becomes an issue at an earlier age. Estimates suggest one in three long-term truants starts out by missing lessons at primary school; almost a third of all pupils picked up on recent truancy sweeps were under the age of 11. In secondary schools, the rate of unauthorized absence has remained unchanged over the past five years and virtually unchanged over the past ten, despite government initiatives and pressure from Ofsted, the national schools inspectorate. All of which suggests truancy is a complex social problem that resists quick fix solutions.

Why do children play truant?

Children picked up on recent sweeps said they'd not gone to school because 'I had to buy a new hamster' or 'I felt I had a spot coming'. Other excuses included 'I don't like Mondays', 'It's my birthday' and, simply, 'It's a Friday'. Psychologists give more complex reasons: bullying, lack of self-esteem, poor teacher–pupil relationships, peer pressure and family problems.

But one complaint stands out: truants usually describe school as boring or irrelevant. For the 14-year-old set on becoming a hairdresser, it can be difficult to see the point of GCSE history. It's no coincidence that countries with a tradition of running a vocational curriculum alongside an academic curriculum have lower rates of non-attendance.

Ticket to truant

Pestering parents until they send you a Jimmy-had-a-migraine note is all well and good – if Jimmy really did have a migraine. But evidence suggests that a substantial number of parents condone their child's non-attendance. For example, most primary-age truants picked up during city centre sweeps are accompanied by a parent. Sometimes parents permit truancy because they want their children to help them or keep them company. Sometimes they just lack the authority to make them attend. In many cases, truancy seems to be as hereditary as brown hair or blue eyes. However, the biggest reason for parental-condoned absence from school needs no psychological explanation: holidays can be 30 per cent cheaper outside peak periods. The problem has escalated to the extent that many schools now list family holidays as the single biggest cause of non-attendance.

The Amos effect

By law, parents are responsible for ensuring that their children attend school. Those who fail can be prosecuted by the local education authority and, if found guilty, face a maximum fine of £2,500 per parent, per child or up to three months in prison. Usually the court opts for a fine, often less than £100, but occasionally parents are jailed in high-profile cases. The first such case was in 2002 when Oxfordshire mother Patricia Amos was jailed for 60 days after two of her five children registered attendance rates of less than 35 per cent. Supporters of the sentence argued that it sent a clear warning to others. Others thought that spending thousands of pounds sending a single mother to prison was unenlightened. The hardliners' argument gained credence when Ms Amos, who served 14 days, admitted the sentence had changed her children's attitudes. Welfare officers and the police reported a drop in truancy cases during the weeks immediately after the case in what became known as 'the Amos effect'.

Since then, however, research has shown that the threat of jail has little long-term effect on truancy levels. Patricia Amos's children, for example, took so little notice of the risk that she was sent to prison again for the same offence two years later. If your school does decide to prosecute, it's unlikely that you will be involved unless you have senior management responsibilities: the decision is usually taken jointly by the school and education welfare officers. For prosecutions to be successful, it's important to have detailed records of all non-attendance, and of all action taken in following up absences. Most LEAs recognize that prosecution can often make matters worse, and use it only as a last resort. But that could change – several authorities have been threatened with legal action by former truants claiming 'educational negligence' because their schools failed to take sufficient action against their parents.

Keeping truants in school – physical and practical

There are all kinds of initiatives around for improving attendance: the challenge is to decide which changes will have most impact for you. Cutting down on post-registration and single-lesson truancy usually calls for practical measures. Think about the premises: take a walk round and keep your eyes open for 'truancy holes' where pupils can slip out of school unnoticed. It's not unheard of for sweeps to pick up a truant in the morning, return him or her to school, then catch the pupil again in the afternoon. Within school try to work out the places where children take refuge once they've skipped lessons. Doing a few spot-checks during your non-teaching lessons could unearth a few surprises. On a more positive note, encourage the school to introduce special facilities for Years 9, 10 and 11 in the same way that sixth-formers get common rooms or break-out spaces.

If pupils still head for town when they should be in your class, don't take it personally! Make sure you are consistent about giving information to the school. If a truancy gets reported to you in any way – from colleagues, from other pupils or from concerned parents – the important thing is to respond. Pass on the facts as soon as you can and don't be afraid to liaise with the local authority, the education welfare team and the police.

Keeping truants in school – academic and pastoral

Depending on what you teach there may be opportunities for introducing discussions about truancy into your lessons, in the same way as raising issues like sex or smoking. English, RE or drama could include discussion about some of the emotional factors, but geography or maths could equally make use of the statistics to raise the subject. Remember, truanting the first time takes courage – but after that it can quickly become a habit. If you can help make pupils aware of truanting and its consequences, then you may well help prevent some pupils taking the first step on the slippery slope.

It's usually activities outside the classroom that have the most effect, however. If you have a pupil who struggles with attendance it might be worth involving them in a mentoring scheme – these have been shown to boost attendance as well as offering useful life skills. Encouraging an involvement in sport, music or drama can also transform a reluctant pupil's attitude to school. If your subject has a practical application then try exploring the possibility of links with tertiary colleges that offer vocational tuition. Even the occasional glimpse of 'real life' can help make classroom learning seem relevant enough to keep a truant in school. In extreme cases, consider getting the pupil and the school to discuss a 'negotiated curriculum', in which truants decide for themselves which lessons they will attend: some school is better than no school. Remember, too, that frequent non-attendance by staff – for whatever reason – can send out the wrong message to pupils. Is every conference, course and training day you sign up for essential?

Finally, make sure you know how to link your pupils to the pastoral support they need. Truants who return to school will need handling with care. If they feel stigmatized, or are subjected to 'enjoy your holiday?'-style sarcasm, chances are they'll be straight back down the shopping centre.

Registration and rapid response

If your school has tried tightening security and relaxing the timetable and is still serious about tackling truancy, you will most likely be asked to look at the way you record and respond to absences. This should have been part of your induction training: if it was overlooked, then ask to be updated.

If you're still ticking names off in old-fashioned registers, then the most effective change is probably the introduction of lesson-by-lesson registration which can detect those who skip the odd period. It might seem time-consuming, but it's important that every teacher is seen to be behind the school's efforts.

Some schools, however, are moving towards using electronic registration systems. These usually operate in one of two ways. One system enables registration to be taken by the teacher using a small notebook-sized computer. The other uses swipe cards that pupils put through a scanner as they enter school buildings or classrooms. In either case, the attendance data is transmitted to a central computer in the school office, and can be processed in minutes.

Modern technology can also help with the next step of contacting parents: many software systems automatically contact parents by phone, text message or e-mail once a child has been logged as out of school. It then leaves a message asking them to record the reason for their child's absence. This kind of automated system frees up administration staff, doesn't get abused by parents and is persistent – even the most obstructive parents tend to get worn down by repeated calls. Schools that have combined electronic registration with an automated response system have been able to cut unauthorized absences by up to 30 per cent. But hi-tech equipment isn't cheap. Electronic registration can cost upwards of £30,000 and despite government funding being made available to equip the most needy schools, fewer than one in three secondary schools have electronic systems.

Ticket to Alton Towers

There are all kinds of carrots to wave alongside the sticks: publishing the names of 100 per cent attenders, awarding certificates, organizing inter-form attendance competitions – go for whatever appeals to pupils. Usually that means a lucrative prize. Think class outings to Alton Towers rather than book tokens or a quaint little trophy. Some schools offer individual prizes, which can be even more enticing, such as an end-of-year trip to Disneyland Paris – to be taken during the holidays, of course – or hold prize draws every week or fortnight, with the names of all 100 per cent attenders going in the hat. You can do your bit by making sure pupils in your classes know you are taking attendance seriously and that good attendance gets noted and rewarded.

Chapter 3
Nits

In the early 1980s, entomologists were boasting that modern medicine would soon make head lice extinct. The same experts now admit there are more head lice in the United Kingdom than at any time in recent history: an estimated one primary age child in five is affected. The independence of modern youngsters – with parents no longer washing and brushing their hair for them – is one factor which helps them flourish. The fashion for soft, spongy hairbrushes rather than old-fashioned combs is another. But perhaps the real reason head lice are thriving is the confusion about what they are, how they spread and how best to get rid of them.

Bed and breakfast

The habitat of *Pediculus capitis* – the head louse – is the human scalp, where they exist as parasites sucking blood through the skin. A nice, warm head also makes a handy incubator for their eggs, which are glued to the hair, close to the scalp surface. When laid, the eggs are about the size of a pinhead and grey, but when they hatch, after about seven days, the empty shell becomes white. Seven days after hatching the new lice start to lay eggs – and the cycle begins again.

Head lice cannot fly or jump, but they're sharp movers, needing only a fleeting moment of direct hair-to-hair contact to move to a new host. This explains why about 80 per cent of all cases occur between the ages of 3 and 12. Secondary pupils may catch head lice from a younger member of the family, but it's in primary schools that lice are rife. Younger children are simply less inhibited when it comes to having their head in contact with another person's.

The long view

Head lice have been around for thousands of years. Dried-up lice have been found on Egyptian mummies, and a set of carved ivory nit combs is believed to date from the twelfth century BC. The history books also propose a wide range of cures. The Romans advocated bathing in viper broth; Victorian mothers would knead children's scalps with their knuckles in a misguided attempt to maim the parasites. But while lice may be one of the ten plagues listed in the Bible, not all civilisations have seen them as a curse. In South America, the Aztecs showed their respect to Montezuma by making offerings of head lice, while traditional Siberian courtship called on young ladies to flick lice from their hair at the man who caught their eye. Today, some tribes in the Middle East deliberately cultivate head lice to harvest them for a nutritious feast.

Dirty lice

Many people still believe head lice are a sign of poor hygiene. The myth sprang up because 'in the old days' working-class families were worst affected, an inevitable result of children sleeping three to a bed. The middle classes were happy to label nits a 'dirty disease' – until they realized their own children were not immune. In the 1980s, a counter-myth began to emerge, with parents of infested children claiming that lice preferred clean hair. In truth, head lice don't care if hair is clean or dirty any more than they worry about whether it's dark or blonde, straight or curly. They simply aren't fussy.

What should I do if there's an outbreak of lice in my school?

Don't panic! The important thing is not to over-react. Lice are not a health threat and are certainly no reason for children to stay away from school. Ideally, lice should be dealt with at home, not at school – the axing of nit nurses was partly an attempt to make parents take responsibility. It's also true that unless the problem is addressed throughout a school, children who get rid of their lice are likely to catch them again within a few weeks.

One strategy is to organize bug-busting weeks when all pupils join a co-ordinated programme of wet-combing on a designated day. This way everyone can shed their nits together, preventing re-infestation. If you plan to do the combing in school, you need parental permission. It may be best to write to parents telling them what you are planning and asking them to reply only if they object.

Why are head lice harmful?

Medically speaking, they aren't. They are an irritant rather than a health hazard – they don't spread disease or cause illness. Physically, the worst that can happen is that children scratch themselves and end up with a secondary infection. But the need to scratch occurs in only one in three cases.

The real problem is not so much *on* the head as *in* the head. Parents in particular can find the notion of head lice distressing, not least because some people can be prone to over-react and see the lice as evidence of bad parenting. Lice can also provide fodder for classroom bullies, or knock the confidence of pupils who might already be struggling with low self-esteem. Being open about the issue and making sure everyone has the facts, rather than feeding on rumours, can help limit the damage.

Nailing lousy myths

Head lice don't leave the head – they can't survive long without blood. So there's no need to fumigate clothes, bedding or toys. Although closely related, head lice are not the same as 'crabs', and don't live in pubic hair. They are specific to humans. You can't catch them from, or pass them on to, family pets.

A 'nit' is the name given to an empty egg shell – not the louse itself. The presence of nits does not necessarily mean the child is infested; the lice may have already moved on.

Alternative alternatives

The internet is crawling with suggested remedies, ranging from mayonnaise to methylated spirits, from vodka to Vaseline. Some of these might actually help – greasy substances weaken the grip of lice, alcohol may kill them – but, unsurprisingly, neither health experts nor hairdressers endorse them. One teacher swears by hairspray. 'It seems to stop them getting a foothold,' she says.

There are also plenty of advertisements for 'natural' solutions made from various combinations of essential oils, with eucalyptus, tea-tree and lavender among the favourites. There is some logic here – plant oils are often natural pesticides secreted to ward off insects. But this means they are sometimes more toxic than man-made chemicals and, unlike the pharmaceutical products, these home-made concoctions have not been subjected to clinical trials.

Perhaps the simplest solution of all is also one of the oldest: when Napoleon's army was bothered by an infestation of nits the order came for every soldier to shave his head. Headteachers might balk at the idea of creating classes of skinheads, but research at the University of Bristol has proved that what worked for Napoleon should work for you too.

Chemical reactions

Most parents' knee-jerk reaction to lice is a trip to the chemist. Here, for between £5 and £10, they can take their pick from a range of shampoos and lotions in which the active ingredient is an agricultural-style insecticide, usually malathion or permethrin. It's the kind of concoction used to treat dog fleas or sheep ticks and, not surprisingly, there are safety concerns about the use of these chemicals in direct contact with children's skin.

There's also a good chance parents will be wasting their money. In the past five years a 'superlouse' has evolved – with bugs in certain parts of the United Kingdom developing immunity to the more popular insecticides, especially permethrin. One GP in Devon recalls his practice giving out 3,000 prescriptions one year 'with little or no impact on the local epidemic'.

Breaking the cycle

The main alternative to chemicals is 'bug-busting'. Developed by the charity Community Hygiene Concern (CHC), it requires a set of specially developed narrow-toothed combs that are used to 'wet-comb' the hair after copious amounts of conditioner have been rubbed in. In dry hair lice can scurry away, but the stickiness of the conditioner stops them in their tracks and allows them to be combed out.

The downside is that to get it right, bug-busting can be a labour-intensive process which needs repeating every fourth day for two weeks. With diligence, however, this should break the nit's life cycle – assuming you haven't missed any, the problem should be solved.

Chapter 4
Bereavement

Almost one in every 30 people will experience the death of a parent before the age of 19. That's roughly one pupil in every class. Many more children will experience the loss of a grandparent, sibling or friend. Growing up is hard enough – lose someone close to you and it can be traumatic. Schools can make a difference when it comes to helping young people cope with bereavement and teachers have a key role to play in the healing process. But how can you help vulnerable pupils through this most bewildering of times?

Do children react to grief differently from adults?

Yes. Adults usually experience grief as a sequence of emotions. Initial shock or numbness is followed by a period of yearning for the deceased, which in turn is replaced by sadness or even depression. Eventually, intense feelings give way to acceptance. Children experience all these emotions – but not necessarily in the same order. Their emotions tend to roller-coaster between the stages.

What's normal?

There is no 'normal' reaction to bereavement. So don't be shocked or surprised by how children react to death. It's not unusual, for example, for younger children to go out and play after hearing of a relative's death. This doesn't mean they're unaffected; it's just an instinctive way of dealing with an emotional crisis. 'Sick' jokes about death are another common defence mechanism.

Even though every situation is unique, it's still possible to identify some typical reactions for different age groups. Under the age of 6, children often view death as temporary or reversible. They might talk about the dead person as if he or she were still alive. It's also common for them to see death as a 'punishment', or feel they may have caused it by their own behaviour. By the age of 7 or 8, most children understand that death is permanent. The death of someone close may cause a preoccupation with matters related to death, and possibly a strong fear of dying. Adolescents usually have an 'adult' understanding of death, but given all the other insecurities teenagers face, their grieving process is often complicated and drawn out. At any age, sadness, anger and guilt are likely to be the dominant emotions. Just as there is no standard way of grieving, so there is no set time limit. But most experts agree that recovery takes at least a year, probably two. And it's not uncommon for bereaved youngsters to suffer from ill health. The death of someone particularly close can weaken the immune system for up to 18 months.

The language of death

When tackling responses to death, it's useful to have a few definitions. Bereavement is the loss through death of a person close to you. Grief is the emotional response to that loss, while mourning is the social expression of grief. All cultures and religions seem to acknowledge that bereavement exists, and in most cases the emotions of grief are similar. But mourning rituals differ widely. Some religions – such as Orthodox Judaism – will hold the funeral service within 24 hours of the death, whereas a Christian ceremony can be more than a week later. Hinduism usually involves two ceremonies, one immediately after the death, the other up to a month later. When dealing with a bereaved pupil, it's important not to impose your own values or beliefs – although that doesn't mean you can't listen carefully and talk about what you believe.

Least said, soonest mended?

Absolutely not. Many teachers worry about saying the wrong thing or reopening emotional wounds. But the biggest mistake is to pretend nothing has happened. Most bereaved children will be itching for the chance to talk and, if not, will soon tell you. But discretion is important. Too much attention may increase an uncomfortable feeling of being different.

Don't worry about not being an expert on bereavement; it may even be an advantage. Use basic counselling techniques – open-ended questions, attentive listening, comments that reflect back the feelings of the child – but, above all, be honest and open. It's not about coming up with answers, it's about being there. Don't be afraid to ask questions, particularly if the child has a faith or culture with which you are unfamiliar. And don't worry if it ends in tears. Short-term upset is better than long-term trauma.

Who should do the talking/listening?

It doesn't matter, as long as somebody does. The responsibility often falls to a form teacher or head of year, but someone else may be more appropriate. The more staff who can make themselves available the better – then it's up to the child who to turn to. Don't be surprised if he or she goes to an unexpected source. One teacher tells how a teenage pupil who was 'really difficult with me – I thought he hated my guts' came to him for support when his father died. Sometimes it's easier for pupils to approach teachers with whom they don't have a rapport, because they feel less exposed.

What if someone from the school dies?

Don't let rumours spread. When a pupil or teacher dies, it's important to keep the whole school properly informed. If the death is sudden, it may be necessary to relax normal routines to give pupils a chance to talk and reflect.

The school's ability to grieve collectively as a community is usually helpful, so it's a good idea to hold an in-school memorial service, in addition to more formal representation at a funeral. Children often find a permanent reminder, such as a tree, bench or memory book, is a useful focus for their feelings. Remember that you and your colleagues will also need time to grieve; sometimes teachers are too busy comforting pupils to confront their own feelings.

Time heals...

Most children eventually move on. But some struggle to come to terms with their loss. Those who have problems with self-esteem are most likely to respond badly. The nature of the death is also a factor. Suicide, murder or violent death are especially difficult, and it may be best to seek professional help immediately – especially if the child has witnessed the death.

Sometimes children will get stuck at one particular stage of the grieving process. Trust your instincts. If things don't seem to be progressing, professional help is probably needed. Warning signs include children continuing to talk as if the dead person is still alive, refusing to talk about them at all, or even talking about wanting to be dead themselves.

What help is available?

The Child Bereavement Trust advises that in nine out of ten cases teachers are in the best position to deal with bereavement. But you still need to know where to turn if you decide outside help is needed. Calling on the National Health Service (services vary from area to area), or an educational psychologist or nurse attached to the school, may be your first option. But several charities offer support for bereaved children. Some will give advice or help with counselling; some specialize in certain situations, such as suicide; others offer general support. Also use your knowledge of affected children. If you know they have a strong religious belief, a leader from their faith may be an appropriate counsellor. Once you've decided who will be providing the support, it's best to stick with them unless there's a problem. Having more than one agency involved can lead to confusion. Above all, if a pupil is referred for specialist help, it's important that you continue to offer support in school.

It happens to us all

We still have hang-ups about death. Often we're just uncomfortable tackling extreme emotions. But, on top of that, death is closely linked to religion and faith, which we tend to think of as private. When we do discuss it, we bring out all sorts of euphemisms – it's hardly surprising if young children get confused. 'Grandma's passed away.' 'When's she coming back?' 'She's gone to a better place.' 'Then why don't we join her?'

Ironically, twenty-first-century children are surrounded by death. But it's only make-believe – playground games, video games, action movies. When people died in their own beds and infant mortality was common, death was a home truth rather than a screen fiction. Bereavement experts have noted that in poorer countries children have fewer problems with death because they are accustomed to seeing dead bodies. Here we tend to try to protect children from that kind of thing, assuming it must be traumatic. In fact, the opposite can be true.

Death education

There are opportunities within the curriculum to explore issues surrounding bereavement. In primaries, the death of a school pet can get discussion moving. Citizenship lessons can easily encompass bereavement – some schools even have mock funerals – and comparing the rituals of various faiths can make a lively RE project. Biology teachers should be aware that teenagers who lose a parent to a tumour or a heart attack will probably be anxious to learn more about the condition. The major bereavement care organizations produce reading lists for English lessons, recommending fiction that deals with death. And never underestimate the value of creative work. Art, drama, English and music all offer opportunities to work through grief, for example, by writing reminiscences of the dead person or creating a work of art in their memory.

What can you do?

All schools should have a bereavement policy that includes a plan of action in the event of an accident involving the death of several pupils as it's difficult to think clearly in the immediate aftermath of a tragedy. It's much more likely, however, that you'll be dealing with individual cases. When a pupil loses a parent or sibling, the most important thing is to keep in contact with the family. This may not be as straightforward as it sounds: unbelievably, some families don't let the school know when a parent has died, or they order the child to keep the death secret. A bereaved child will usually be kept at home for a few days, but it may be best not to let this continue for too long. School can be a positive force in the grieving process – children find the routine comforting. It also gives them the chance to talk to people unaffected by the bereavement. Try to have a system to remind you when the anniversary of a bereavement is approaching so you are aware of potentially sensitive situations.

Off the rails

Bereaved children are often the first to throw a punch in the playground, as an outlet for the anger they feel. Don't make excuses for poor behaviour. It's important to be sympathetic, but it's still best to tackle unacceptable behaviour as you usually would. The same is true of poor academic work. Studies have shown that many children who lose a parent go on to suffer emotional and learning difficulties. Concentration levels will dip and it's easy for a child to lose confidence or interest. Don't make too many allowances, however. Beginning an end-of-term report with 'considering the difficult circumstances' can establish a pattern of under-achievement.

Problems can be particularly acute when children are struggling to come to terms with the loss of a parent. Often it's not only their own grief which troubles them, but also that of the surviving parent. The children's telephone helpline, ChildLine, reports a significant number of calls ostensibly about neglect, abuse or a parent's drinking – but where the surviving parent's failure to cope with bereavement turns out to be at the core of the issue. The loss of a parent can also mean big changes in lifestyle, particularly for an adolescent suddenly charged with looking after siblings or trying to earn part-time cash. Sometimes problems in school are not a result of personal grief, but of the practical adjustments brought about by bereavement.

Degrees of grief

Most of us probably think in terms of a scale of bereavement. So losing a parent, for example, comes higher up the list than losing a grandparent. Forget such assumptions with children. A grandparent's death is often a child's first experience of bereavement – and the loss can be devastating. For Muslims, in particular, the extended family is often close-knit, so don't be surprised to see a strong reaction to the death of an aunt or cousin. The important thing is to respond to how someone is feeling, not how you think they should be feeling.

Chapter 5
Junk food

Free fruit in primary schools. A ban on the sale of crisps and pop and sweets. Bigger spending on healthier school meals. A children's manifesto to halt the rise of obesity by 2010. The government seems serious about tackling children's nutrition. But is that enough to curb the appetite for junk food? With mounting evidence that what children eat can affect the way they learn and behave, it's in every teacher's interest to keep an eye on the mounting pile of crisp packets and drink cans cluttering the classroom.

Not just junk?

Many of the foods we now think of as 'junk' started life with a more positive image. Sweets often evolved from nineteenth-century throat treatments and manufacturers of fizzy drinks like Coca-Cola, Pepsi and Lucozade also emphasized the medicinal benefits of their products in early marketing. In the days when people generally consumed less sugar and caffeine, the pick-me-up qualities were a big selling point: Lucozade, it was claimed, 'aids recovery', while Pepsi, invented by an American pharmacist in 1893, was considered both refreshing and stimulating. Original American hamburgers, invented around 1900, were made of lean beef, broiled rather than fried, and served in dry toast. No ketchup, mustard, mayo or cheese. And the workers in England's industrial towns were sustained on nourishing, good-value fish and chip meals from the 1860s when the first shops opened.

In the twentieth century, processed foods like Spam were an important source of protein for many families during and after the war. Chocolate, too, was often considered to provide much-needed milk for children – remember the 'glass and a half in every bar'? It has only been over recent decades that an occasional treat has turned into a daily meal. Which is where the problems start.

What's in a name?

We all think we recognize junk food when we see it – a bag of crisps, a fizzy drink, something with chocolate. But what about a low-fat pre-packed sandwich? Junk or convenient? And a take-away pizza? A home-baked cake? No-one seems to know where the term 'junk food' originated, but it's generally agreed that it defines any food with little or no nutrients but an excess of fat and calories. Often this means heavily processed food, but it doesn't necessarily exclude meals served up at home or school. Pre-packaged food from the supermarket or catering portions of school meal favourites can live up to the junk-food label just as easily as a quick meal at the local takeaway. A study by the Soil Association in 2004 found that a primary school child eating five school meals a week was getting 40 per cent more salt, 28 per cent more saturated fat and 20 per cent more sugar than the recommended amounts.

When it comes to introducing guidelines on, for example, promoting junk food in schools or getting better nutrition labelling, getting an agreed definition on what constitutes 'junk' can be tricky. However, in 2005 the government issued a series of new guidelines aimed at reducing the amount of junk food in schools and increasing the nutritional value of school meals. A review panel, commissioned to look at exactly what children were eating, suggested school meals should be monitored for basic nutrients and how much fat, sugar, protein and fibre they contain. Kitchens should be updated so that meals can be prepared on site from fresh, local ingredients and tuck shops and vending machines should be subject to new, tougher nutritional standards. The vision was that by the end of 2006 junk food would have been phased out of school life and by 2008 (for primaries) and 2009 (for secondaries) all school meals would be vitamin-rich, low-fat and generally healthy. Even so, some campaigners would like to see the criteria for school meals broadened yet further to include things like residues from agriculture and pesticides, additives and preservatives, and production techniques like genetic modification.

The junk food habit

Children are eating more junk food than ever – the equivalent of eight chocolate bars a day more than their grandparents. The government's National Diet and Nutrition Survey in 2000 found that 70 per cent of primary school children regularly guzzle fizzy drinks – on average getting through 30 glasses a week – and 92 per cent of 4–18-year-olds eat more than recommended adult levels of saturated fat. More worryingly, healthier alternatives are getting edged out. Figures from the Department of Health in 2004 suggested that, despite all the healthy eating campaigns, only one in nine children eats five daily portions of fruit and vegetables, and many are still eating none.

One reason why habits are proving so hard to change may be the addictive nature of junk food. At Oxford University, research by the Food and Behaviour Research Group (FAB) has found that rats can become addicted to high-sugar diets and experience withdrawal symptoms if their sugar fix is reduced. No wonder children can get jumpy at the end of a long sugar-free lesson! At Wisconsin University in America, researchers also found that a good helping of junk food releases chemicals called opioids into the brain: the same chemicals that play a major part in drug or alcohol addiction.

Getting super-sized

Kicking the junk food habit is not easy. Loyalty marketing schemes encourage us to keep going back for more while financial incentives prompt us to 'super-size' to bigger portions. And the very nature of junk food makes it difficult for the body to know when enough is enough. According to research at the Human Nutrition Research Centre at the University of Cambridge, junk food has a high 'energy density' – the amount of calories it contains in proportion to its weight. This throws our appetite control systems into disarray. Our appetite tells us we need to eat more to make us feel full, but then we end up eating far more calories than our body intended.

This is a particular problem for children: not only are their energy needs lower, but the calories in a double cheeseburger are proportionally higher for them than for, say, a six-foot rugby player. The Cambridge research found that typical menus at McDonalds, KFC and Burger King contained 65 per cent more calories per bite than an average British meal and more than twice that of a recommended healthy diet. Which means a child tucking into a Big Mac and fries at lunchtime will eat almost twice as many calories as one eating the same weight of pasta and salad.

A body of evidence...

Think of junk food and you think of America: a study in 2000 found that a third of the average American diet consisted of junk food, while recent publicity for the wildlife department in Colorado had to explain the dangers of leaving out hamburgers for wild mountain lions.

But lifestyle changes throughout the world mean that junk food is a growing problem almost everywhere. It is estimated that a quarter of all EU children are now obese, and even countries which, until recently, had traditionally provided healthy home-cooked meals are turning to quicker, more highly processed alternatives. The International Obesity Taskforce recently found that over a third of Italian 9-year-olds and 27 per cent of Spanish children are overweight. While in France, the government is so worried about the spread of the junk-food habit that it has banned vending machines from schools and introduced health warnings on advertising for certain foods.

In the United Kingdom, the rapid rise in rates of childhood obesity has also been making the headlines. According to the Medical Research Council, the number of obese 6-year-olds has doubled in Britain over the last ten years, with numbers trebling for 15-year-olds. One in five children is now considered obese. And while most children are still not fat, changing eating habits mean nearly all are at risk of becoming fat. Indulging in just 200 g (7 oz) of junk food, or a couple of burgers, twice a week means an extra 250,000 kJ (or 59,808 calories) a year which is enough to put on almost 8 kg (17.6 lb). Even if a junk food diet doesn't lead directly to obesity, poor nutrition can sow the early seeds for a whole range of conditions from heart disease to asthma or cancer. Type two diabetes, usually only associated with adults and caused by poor diet, has become evident in children for the first time during the past few years.

...Or all in the mind?

Less well-publicized than the physical effects of a junk food diet, however, are the links between nutrition and mental health. The artificial high caused by the sugar content of fizzy drinks, for example, plays havoc with blood-sugar levels which in turn affects concentration and mood. Anecdotal evidence from experienced teachers that children's behaviour can deteriorate after break-time snacking is beginning to be explored by researchers keen to see whether the chemically-produced hydrogenated fats in crisps and biscuits can change the way the brain works. All of which means that anything from tearful tantrums to hyperactivity could be linked to poor nutrition.

A report published by the University of Florida in 2005 found that some school districts in America routinely alter the content of school lunches on test days to get better results. Calorie intake varied from 737 per student per lunch on normal days to 825 on a test day, adding up to 8 per cent more calories. Correspondingly, grades for those pupils getting the energy boost rose by 7 per cent in mathematics and 4 per cent in English. But nutrition is, of course, about more than simply extra calories. Take a modest mineral like zinc, for example. A survey of UK school children undertaken by the Consumers' Association in 2003 found that almost half were deficient in zinc which would mean a reduced ability to taste and smell and so prompt cravings for very sweet, salty or spicy foods. Research at the Human Nutrition Research Centre in North Dakota has found that a daily supplement of zinc can boost the performance of 12–13-year-olds in school by improving the ability to concentrate, enhancing memory and increasing attention levels. Meanwhile, closer to home, the Food and Behaviour Research Group at the University of Oxford has been tracking a whole range of links between a healthy diet and a healthy brain. Its research has shown that everything from learning to mood and behaviour can be improved by better nutrition.

Forbidden fruit

The first step in getting children into healthier eating habits is to help them to understand the choices they make. This is about more than examining what's in front of them on the plate; it's about making connections between what's picked off the supermarket shelf, what's taught in the classroom and what's served up in the dining room. Some schools have experimented with taking classes on shopping trips to food suppliers or to organic farms; exploring dining etiquette for different cultures; having pupils help out in the kitchens or even having occasional meals cooked entirely by teams of (supervised) children. Recent government guidelines have also pushed for all children to learn practical cookery in school. Whatever the activity, the key is in helping children find an interest in what they eat, and feel confident enough to enjoy food as a social event. In time this should help stem the tide to the takeaway and break the cycle of reliance on processed food.

Most experts agree that basic education in nutrition cannot begin too soon. Getting the message across at nursery and primary level is important in forming healthy eating habits, particularly since rebel teenagers can be tempted to resist nutritional advice. The Social Issues Research Centre in Oxford has found that some young people use junk food as a form of protest, like smoking. They choose the greasy sausage roll not because it tastes good but because they know what they are eating is considered 'bad' and choose deliberately to fly in the face of the healthy-eating mantra. It's the shock value, rather than the flavour, which appeals.

In the balance

Many nutritionists would argue there's no such thing as bad food, only a bad diet. The key lies in getting a balance between what we fancy and what's good for us. While exactly what's cooked up in the school kitchens may be outside your control, every classroom can do its bit to help change attitudes to eating. Because in the end, it may be ways of thinking about food, rather than just the food itself, which need to change. It's all too easy, for example, to set up positive associations about junk food that are hard to break: where do your pupils get taken for their treats? To a fast-food restaurant? It's because of these kind of ingrained habits, that schools which have run successful healthy-eating campaigns strongly recommend getting everyone involved from governors to parents. If the parent teacher association is holding a barbeque make sure there's a big attractive salad and some strawberries. Or how about a healthy hamper in the Christmas raffle? One teacher who had previously been strict about eating in class, began to allow children to snack in his lessons – as long as they were eating a piece of fruit. The intake of vitamins soon rocketed!

In practice

The Shropshire 'Local and Healthy Food for Schools' project came about because we were concerned about poor, junk-food diets. We want to encourage healthier living and eating. We know this has knock-on effects on everything from social skills to learning. In addition, there's a practical element: many of our schools serve farming families and we want to boost the local agricultural economy by sourcing food as locally as possible, in some cases from the field next door.

In the summer term of 2004 we looked at the nutritional content of the menus in all the schools in Shropshire. This quite literally meant rummaging through kitchen cupboards and scrutinising product information from suppliers. We employed a qualified nutritionist to advise on healthier menus. These were introduced into all Shropshire primary schools in September 2004 after discussions with teachers, parents and pupils.

The basic principle is to reduce the amount of processed foods with high levels of fat, sugar and salt. Instead we want to focus on healthier cooking methods and to increase fresh fruit and vegetables; seasonal and local produce, and non-refined carbohydrates. We have also banned certain additives. Our old menus were rotated on a four-weekly system right through the school year. This meant that something like cauliflower had to be available for the entire 39 weeks. By introducing seasonal ingredients in the new menus we can use local produce at its freshest and cheapest. Six primary schools have also worked with the Soil Association to use organic ingredients wherever possible, and to make cooked dishes and puddings from scratch.

We want to try to understand the problems involved in getting local produce into the system. The wholesaler pointed out, for example, that produce shelf life has to be guaranteed for seven days because many schools only have one weekly delivery and don't have chill store rooms. This can have a knock-on effect on the type of foods we offer: processed foods with additives can keep more reliably for longer.

The staff employed in our school kitchens are one of our biggest assets. They're proud of their food and are on the front line influencing the choices children make. They formed a School Cooks group looking at menus, trying new products and talking to parents and pupils. We organized training days with the Soil Association and visits to other schools. We also offer a foundation course in basic nutrition to all cooks and assistant cooks throughout the county. So far over 25 staff have completed the course.

We have tried changing menus in the past but it proved unpopular: children struggled to accept foods they didn't recognize from home. Numbers eating school meals fell and the old 'junk food' options were brought back. We've learnt that change must go hand-in-hand with educational work. So we've developed healthy-eating activities linked to the PHSE curriculum. We've also worked hard with parents through workshops and events. The dangers of junk food diets have received a lot of media attention recently and parents have been given a lot of generalized information about school meals. We want them to understand what we're trying to do differently, so that they can be confident their children are getting good food and they're getting good value.

We've made a lot of progress in a short time: 95 per cent of our fresh meat is sourced from Shropshire, for example, and most of our fruit and vegetables come from local farm shops. Feedback from parents, teachers and staff has been encouraging. But some of the children still need convincing! Because we've cut back on popular, familiar items, like nuggets and chips, meal uptake has not increased as much as we would like. But we're taking a long-term view and believe that, given time, numbers will increase. It's not only about changing eating habits – it's about improving quality of life for everybody.

Bill Campbell is operations manager for Shire Services, Shropshire County Council's school meals provider.

Chapter 6
Homophobia

It's difficult to say how many lesbian, gay, bisexual and transsexual teachers there are, but it has been estimated by some groups that the figure is about 50,000. Meanwhile, around one in 10 pupils may be homosexual. Yet although 80 per cent of schools say they are aware of incidents of homophobic bullying, only 6 per cent have a policy to deal with it. Which means a significant proportion of the school community is faced with a hostile, even violent environment – and little protection. New laws banning homophobic discrimination in the workplace give gay teachers some safeguards, but does this make a difference if you're faced with a class of bigots? And with almost all gay young people suffering verbal abuse, how can you make sure homophobic language doesn't go unchallenged?

Hasn't Section 28 been repealed?

Yes. Section 28 of the Local Government Act (1998) was repealed in Scotland in 2000 and in England and Wales in November 2003. It banned local authorities from promoting 'the acceptability of homosexuality as a pretended family relationship'. Although it had never applied directly to individual schools, many teachers were confused about what the Act allowed, and felt unable to deal confidently with homophobic bullying. And many remain unaware that the law has changed. While the introduction of Section 28 tended to get plenty of publicity, it's repeal was a much quieter affair, so some schools are not quite sure of its current status.

The Employment Equality (Sexual Orientation) Regulation, in force since December 2003, outlaws any discrimination or harassment in the workplace on the grounds of perceived or actual sexual orientation; and harassment includes creating a hostile environment or making it difficult for a gay person to come out. Although these things can be slow to take effect, there is some evidence that this has already had profound implications for homophobia, giving gay people the same rights as other workers and beginning to overcome some of the ambiguity and prejudice around homosexuality.

Does homophobia affect my school?

Every large secondary school is likely to have a significant number of homosexual staff and pupils. In a national survey of sexual attitudes and lifestyles between 1999 and 2001, just over 8 per cent of the 11,000 people questioned had experienced some kind of sexual activity with someone of the same gender. Among school-age young people, more than 1 per cent of boys and 5 per cent of girls had experienced some form of homosexual activity, and more reported homosexual attraction. The stigma attached to admitting homosexuality means these figures are likely to be conservative.

Young people are more likely than adults to be the victims of extreme homophobia. In research carried out by the gay rights group Stonewall, 90 per cent of respondents had been verbally assaulted and almost 50 per cent physically attacked while they were young, with half of attacks happening at school perpetrated by fellow students. These are not only shocking statistics: they illustrate ingrained prejudice in schools.

Faith schools

Homosexuality can be a particularly tricky issue for faith schools. They usually demonstrate the strongest resistance to tackling homophobia, often as part of a tough line on sexuality in general. Exploring sexuality can be difficult for gay young people from strong religious backgrounds, particularly if it means a break with family and friends. Without school support, they risk isolation, depression and self harm.

Denominational schools may also be equivocal about employing openly gay teachers. If you're applying for jobs at faith schools and think it might be an issue, then as with all jobs, it's worth doing some proper research into the school environment (and the unspoken do's and don'ts) before jumping into a new post.

Sticks and stones

Homophobic bullying, like other kinds of bullying, can take many forms, from stares in the corridor to the vandalizing of personal property and physical attack. But homophobia has one extra weapon: ingrained language habits. Ofsted highlights derogatory use of homophobic language in its reports, but 'gay' is still routinely used as an insult. Studies have shown that perceived homosexuality is the second most likely trigger for bullying (after weight), and that the rate of suicide and self harm among gay and lesbian adolescents is two to three times higher than for their heterosexual peers. Homosexual young people have to face everything from ignorance to open hostility and, unsurprisingly, often become long-term truants.

If you are a gay member of staff, homophobic bullying can make an already demanding job impossible. Most gay teachers don't come out in schools, and for good reason. 'It's not those I teach who give me problems,' says a gay teacher from Wales. 'It's those I don't teach. I've had a poster campaign against me in the school corridors, e-mails accusing me of paedophilia, abuse in the streets, parents refusing to talk to me. A week doesn't go by without vicious verbal abuse, although I've never been physically attacked. Yet.'

Different needs

Homophobia throws up all sorts of anomalies. In particular, attitudes towards gay men and lesbians can vary. Lesbianism is often presented as sexy and unthreatening whereas gay men tend to be stuck with an image that is either comically effete or rapaciously sexual. Close friendships between girls of school age are encouraged, and displays of affection are an acceptable part of young female bonding. Boys face much more pressure to be physically discreet.

When it comes to teaching, however, it's often lesbians who get a hard time. The stereotypical gay man is sweet, sensitive and caring – the kind of qualities teachers are supposed to ooze in abundance. Whereas the stereotypical lesbian remains difficult, man-hating and butch: the last person anyone wants teaching their children.

The problem can also vary depending on where you live. Many urban centres have thriving and highly visible gay communities where information and social networks are well established. Facilities tend to be poorer in rural areas. Then there's the spectre of village gossip. In small communities without much social mobility, local habits of thought and speech can go unchallenged for decades. Trying to change behaviour can be particularly daunting for someone in a small village and rural schools can face particular problems in challenging issues such as homophobic language.

Why are schools so slow to change?

Recent surveys about social attitudes have shown increasingly liberal views about homosexuality, particularly among under-50s. But this is rarely reflected in schools. Research has shown that failure to act is usually a combination of lack of awareness and an absence of staff willing to take on the job. Often it takes an extraordinary event, such as someone coming out, to bring the issues into the open.

In fact, of course, homophobia is no different from an issue like racism which has been dealt with in most schools for years. Yet most teachers still seem to feel more comfortable challenging someone about an overtly racist remark than an openly homophobic one.

So what can be done?

It can be tempting to start the ball rolling by bringing someone into the classroom with a new point of view. Some teachers have successfully built lessons around conversations with a gay or HIV-positive gay man. But you need to be careful. Unless this kind of event is part of a wider, long-term strategy it can end up being little more than a freak show. Most specialists advise tackling homophobia as part of a holistic approach to improving the school environment – which might also include raising issues about race, gender or religion – rather than highlighting it as a stand-alone problem.

Using your Healthy Schools co-ordinator can be a good start. They should have experience of the issues and can help you draw up a schedule that includes everything from getting homophobia into the management agenda to working on partnerships with parents. It may also be worth taking time to collect evidence. A series of simple questionnaires to parents, staff and pupils can highlight something like the use of homophobic language and give you proof that it needs to be tackled. Even at primary level, there's lots of basic groundwork that can be done in teaching citizenship, decency and tolerance.

And in the staffroom?

Because raising issues about homosexuality can incite powerful reactions, it's important that it's not left to a few teachers while the rest of the staffroom looks the other way. Nor should it be assumed that gay staff will be in the front line. Many feel resentful of being used as a lever to get difficult issues out in the open. But the thought of wading in on a crusade against ingrained homophobia can be a frightening one. You may feel it's not something you are qualified to deal with, and asking for training before you start is a good way of boosting confidence as well as skills. You may also find it helpful to plan to take sessions in teams rather than taking a class on your own. Calling in support from a specialist organization may be a good introduction, but experts stress that, in the end, it's up to the school and its staff to take responsibility for a coherent, integrated approach.

It may not just be pupils' attitudes that need addressing. Staff at fpa Scotland (formerly the Family Planning Association), working on sexual health issues with young people were 'surprised' at the number of times pupils raised concerns about the level of homophobia from teachers. And few gay teachers feel comfortable about coming out to their colleagues – or their bosses. A recent NASUWT survey identified homophobic bullying as a significant part of management bullying.

What's being done to help?

Partnership projects involving voluntary organizations, charities, unions and the police are gradually raising awareness and offering strategies for tackling homophobia. Some of these projects are aimed directly at schools. Several resource packs aim to create a basic structure for action, and many of the specialist organizations work in schools or train teachers in an attempt to chip away at entrenched attitudes.

Education for All represents a broad coalition of national and devolved government, universities, unions and all the major charities working with gay young people. Managed by Stonewall and Families and Friends of Lesbians and Gay Men (Fflag), the campaign airs the issues around homophobia as well as collates research and evidence, and provides resources and practical advice for dealing with homophobia in schools.

Meanwhile, teaching unions report growing numbers of members asking for advice and support, and most now have specialist teams to help you if you need it. They can be particularly helpful if you feel homophobia has contributed to issues of recruitment or redundancy. As well as publishing advice documents, they run conferences and seminars that address issues raised by members and offer practical solutions.

Chapter 7
Self harm

Research published in January 2005 by the National Inquiry into Self Harm, found that one in ten 15–16-year-olds had deliberately hurt themselves. A year earlier, an NHS agency had warned that self harm was reaching 'epidemic' proportions, with growing numbers admitted to hospital casualty departments. The problem can be particularly difficult to tackle in schools, where teenage girls have been known to set up 'cutting clubs' at break, and where you can find yourself bewildered and disgusted by children who deliberately hurt themselves.

What is self harm?

Self harm is the term used to describe deliberately injuring yourself. The most common method is by repeatedly cutting the skin (usually the arms or legs) with knives, razor blades or scissors. But some people burn or scald themselves, pull out hair or eyelashes, jump from heights, strangle themselves, swallow sharp objects or take poisons. Often people try a combination of techniques. And at the extreme end of the scale, self-harmers gouge out eyes or amputate nipples or fingers.

A particular problem for schools?

The figures for self harm appear to be rising alarmingly – and young people are particularly at risk. Around 24,000 people a year under the age of 18 are treated in hospital casualty departments because of deliberate self-inflicted injuries. But this may be only about a tenth of the numbers affected. Most people self harm in private, and many don't seek medical help. Government research in 2002 found that 215,000 11–15-year-olds may have harmed themselves at some time, and recent figures from ChildLine show that calls about self harm have increased by around 65 per cent in two years. All of which suggests that, in an average class of 20 pupils, two will deliberately harm themselves during their teen years. Nor is it just a problem for secondaries to worry about: the National Inquiry into Self Harm found that children as young as 5 could be deliberately banging their heads or grazing their knees in the playground. It can be difficult to tell for sure whether self harm is growing or whether there are just more people seeking support, but organizations like the National Self Harm Network report that around half of their work is with young people.

Who is most at risk?

There is no one type of self-harmer: it's difficult to look for risk factors and then find a target group. But the figures show that girls are more likely to self harm than boys: a study of 15- and 16-year-olds carried out by department of psychiatry researchers at Oxford University in 2002 found that girls were four times more likely than boys to deliberately hurt themselves. The rate is particularly high for girls living with one parent, and Asian girls, though no-one is yet sure why. Self harm is more common among those who have been bullied and is strongly associated with physical and sexual abuse. Recent evidence also suggests a strong link between self harm and poverty. But it's not just an issue for teenage girls: figures collated by North Lanarkshire schools between 1999 and 2002, for example, found that at primary level boys were more likely to harm themselves than girls.

Why do it?

Just as there's no simple formula for working out who might self harm, so the reasons why young people do it are often complicated. The idea that it's a thrill-seeking 'cutting craze' is wrong: it's much more likely to be connected to long-term distress. In a research project carried out in 2002 by children's charity nch (formerly the National Children's Home), all the young people interviewed said their self injury was a result of childhood traumas including rape, unwanted pregnancy, bullying, parental divorce and bereavement. Exam stress, relationship problems, worries about sexual identity, perceived pressure from parents and lack of self-confidence can also have a role to play.

Contrary to popular myth, self harm is not an attention-seeking ploy, or a cry for help. Most cases take place hidden away in bedrooms or school toilets, and most young people are careful to cover the evidence. And despite the fact that, statistically, those who self harm are 100 times more likely to go on to commit suicide than those who do not, most young people who hurt themselves are not suicidal but are simply trying to cope with their feelings.

Some specialists also suggest that self-harmers are often bad at social problem-solving. When things go wrong with family or friends, they find it hard to find positive ways of dealing with their anguish – and so resort instead to dysfunctional ways of coping.

The feel-good factor

There are, though, some common factors which help explain why young people self harm. Many say it makes them feel more in control. Research has shown that one common trait, for example, is careful preparation and cleaning up – having tissues, antiseptic and plasters to hand and following a well-rehearsed routine. Others report feelings of overwhelming relief from their problems or suggest it makes them feel more alive.

But the reasons why someone starts self-harming may be different from why they keep on doing it. Just like alcohol or drugs, self harm is addictive. When we feel pain our bodies release endorphins, natural morphine-like chemicals which act as painkillers, and which account for why many people say they feel euphoric after hurting themselves. Those who self harm repeatedly could well be addicted to this rush of endorphins.

Keeping quiet...

Young people who self harm are often wary of going to hospital. And their fears may not be ungrounded. A report in 2004 by the National Institute for Clinical Excellence found that half of those seeking treatment for self-harm injuries received no follow-up care or psychological assessment, while some NHS staff – especially in overworked A&E departments – were unsympathetic. In extreme cases, doctors had stitched up self-inflicted wounds without anaesthetic.

But schools are not much higher on the list of potential confidantes. Statistics from the Samaritans and the Centre for Suicide Research at Oxford University show that nearly half of young people have tried to find help from someone before hurting themselves – but that they find it difficult to talk to teachers because they are too embarrassed, or feel their problem is not important enough. Others are worried that a word in the ear of a favourite teacher may soon become a painful 'official' experience: one girl found with lacerated arms was repeatedly asked to dredge up her worries to the PE teacher (who discovered the cuts), then her year tutor, pastoral head, head teacher, school nurse and, finally, a community paediatrician. Often the self-harmer simply doesn't know how to describe what they're feeling. It's because they can't talk about it that they are cutting themselves. As a teacher, the instinctive reaction is to take away the knife – but it's worth remembering that it also removes one way for the child to cope.

...or speaking out?

Despite not necessarily wanting to talk about their own case, a recent poll of young people on a self harm web forum showed that 82 per cent of respondents would like self harm discussed more openly in their schools. And while some said it was a subject they had covered in personal social and health education (PSHE), others said it was something they had to find out the hard way from their own or a friend's experience. Self harm is rarely covered specifically by initiatives like the Healthy Schools Standard or the DfES Healthy Living Blueprint and there has long been a need for more open discussion and better training for teachers. But some experts warn that it can be a fine line between putting ideas into some pupils' heads and providing necessary information. In some cases, self harm can be catching, so it's important not to glamorize it. Bringing self harm into the open should be about trying to make the behaviour seem more normal, not a bit of a thrill – it might be helpful to think of it in the same spectrum as other behaviour that is not necessarily good for young people, like unprotected sex or binge drinking.

Schools which are tackling the problem often put staff training top of the list. Would you know how to spot telltale signs – like someone wearing long sleeves on a stinking hot day – and how to access local support services? But alongside the practical stuff, it's also important to be prepared for the distressing nature of self harm. It's quite common to feel a good deal of revulsion when you start tackling the issue, but it's important not to let these feelings show.

You are not alone

Because the issues underlying self harm are so complex and varied, the 'right' response will often vary from case to case. It should be unique to each person. Some self-harmers might need to be put in touch with services like helplines or web forums, some might want hands-on, face-to-face support. Many self harm support groups offer personal e-mail support, and this has proved particularly popular with young people, some of whom might be blocked from using online self-help forums by parental control facilities on their computers. The best advice, however, is to start with the basics. A bit of kindness and sensitivity can go a long way. Taking time to listen and making someone feel valued is always a good starting point – it's important not to see someone who self harms as a problem, because that negativity will feed back. Even if you're nervous about saying or doing the right thing, it's worth making some kind of intervention. A few kind words – even if you end up saying the wrong thing in the right way – can have a massive impact on breaking the cycle of harm. But be aware of your limitations: if you don't feel able to cope with a case, then seek support.

Home truths

Most specialists believe the best way to deal with self harm is to take a whole school approach which offers everyone – staff, students and parents – the chance to develop effective ways of coping with stress, anxiety and unhappiness. This may include anything from developing communication and social skills through 'circle time' to finding ways of improving self esteem and positive thinking. Peer support programmes, like buddy schemes, are also important because many self-harmers prefer to confide in someone their own age.

But whatever steps you take at school, there's still bound to be knock-on effects from home, and many teachers report difficulties in getting help from parents in tackling self harm. Sometimes parents are unwilling to admit there's a problem, and refuse to seek professional advice. And sometimes they don't want difficulties at home – which may be one of the underlying causes of the self harm – to come into the open. Just as importantly, many young people don't want their parents involved. While many schools have a policy of informing parents as soon as a self harm case is discovered, many specialists claim that talking to parents can be damaging and advise dealing with the self-harmer in confidence.

In the fold

Getting professional support to tackle self harm is not always easy. Many schools lack funding for specialist posts like a school nurse, while voluntary organizations can be overwhelmed with calls for help. Some LEAs are beginning to tackle self harm in partnership with specialists like educational psychologists and youth social workers, but training provision for individual teachers is patchy. There are, however, some basics which can be helpful while you're waiting for a more structured programme of support. Making sure you and your colleagues are aware of potential triggers for self harm, like transition to senior school, options and exams, is a good start. Teenagers interviewed by the National Inquiry into Self Harm also recommended simple measures like covering self harm in school magazines, providing a free telephone link to a support organization or offering first-aid equipment for students to treat their own wounds. If you do discover a case, the important thing is not to focus on the injuries, but on the underlying problems: too much attention to the cuts and bruises might just encourage someone to repeat the harming. Many specialists also advise trying to find alternatives to excluding a self-harmer, even if they are consistently found in school with a knife: by keeping a child at home, you are possibly removing them from their most important source of safety and security. For many young self-harmers, being part of the school network is what keeps them going.

Not all bad news

There's no easy 'cure' for self harm: there is plenty of evidence from 50- and 60-year-olds who still resort to hurting themselves in times of particular stress. But experts suggests that an increasing willingness to talk about the problem should help young people feel less isolated and give them more information about support networks. In the long term this should mean friends and family are more aware and open to talking about the problems underlying self harm, even if they struggle to deal with the self harm itself. And many teenagers show impressive commitment, and ingenuity, in trying to stop themselves self harming – recent postings to a self harm web forum included '115 things to do instead of self harming', advocating distractions such as playing online scrabble.

It can also be encouraging to listen to some of the stories young people tell about self-harming, which often emphasize issues of self-protection, rather than self-destruction. It's easy to get hung up on the negatives of self harm, but believe it or not there are some positives: the young person is still alive and is still trying to find a way to cope.

Chapter 8
Teenage suicide

Every year, about 300 young people commit suicide, making it the second most common cause of death after road accidents among 16–19-year-olds. And for every youngster who takes his or her own life, many more attempt to do so. The figures add up to a lot of teenagers trying to cope with distress, frustration and feelings of hopelessness. Knowing how to recognize vulnerable students and what you can do to help – as well as being prepared to cope with the aftermath if the unthinkable does happen – can be useful knowledge when you end up with only a moment or two to make an intervention.

Are teenagers particularly vulnerable?

Although people of all ages and backgrounds take their own lives, suicide rates and diagnoses of depression in young people have risen steadily since 1970. It is older teenagers who are most at risk; until the age of 14, suicide is relatively uncommon, though there are still around 20 cases every year.

The factors are complicated, but some common elements help to suggest why adolescents may be vulnerable. Because teenagers don't have much life experience, they can easily perceive a stressful situation as inescapable and turn to short-term avoiding strategies, like drink or drugs, to help. In turn this gets them into even more trouble. Young people can also be social perfectionists with unrealistic expectations of themselves. Any knock-back can leave them feeling a failure.

While suicide may not be linked directly to adolescence, it is linked to periods of transition. If you consider the stresses of changing family relationships, physical development, the discovery of romance and sex, and nervousness about making your own way in the world beyond school, then you can begin to see why young people may be at risk.

What causes someone to commit suicide?

Suicide rarely has a single cause. It's usually the result of a complex combination of circumstances, which the Trust for the Study of Adolescence has divided into 'primary' and 'secondary' risk factors. The primary, or more serious, factors include psychiatric disorder, a previous suicide attempt, serious depression and drug or alcohol abuse. Secondary risk factors include a family history of suicide, the suicide of a friend or a significant blow to self-esteem. Even knowing these factors, however, it can be incredibly difficult to pin down a specific risk: looking back with hindsight it may be almost impossible to have known someone would commit suicide.

One common element associated with suicide risk, however, is hopelessness. More than 90 per cent of suicidal people admit to feeling they have no hope for the future. Teenagers who find problem-solving difficult, particularly when it comes to personal issues, often get sucked into feelings of desperation. They tend to be poor at solving social problems, like a relationship crisis, and have fewer and less appropriate solutions to offer. Soon, they begin to feel very alone and feelings of isolation are closely linked to depression and suicide. Increased suicide risks have been seen in teenagers isolated from their families in custody or care, and in gay, lesbian or bisexual young people who have difficulty getting emotional support from their families. Bullying, too, is an important factor; bullied young people often report feelings of isolation and are in the suicide 'at risk' group.

What's the relationship between self harm and suicide?

Teenagers who self harm are more than 100 times more likely to go on to commit suicide than those who don't. Many teenagers who self harm report feeling lost in a system that doesn't care, where nobody wants to talk to them. But it should not be assumed that someone who self harms is a suicide risk. For some young people, self harm allows them to cope with their feelings to such an extent that they are actually less likely to go on to kill themselves.

Boys and girls, north and south

One of the reasons it is so difficult to identify factors in teenage suicide is the huge variation between the rates for young men and those for young women. Fifteen per 100,000 young men (15–24-year-olds) in England and Wales kill themselves each year, while the figure for young women is four per 100,000. In contrast, attempted suicide and deliberate self harm are more common for girls. There is no definitive reason for the difference, but research has shown that young men may be more affected by unemployment or poor employment opportunities, may find accessing health services more difficult, and may have greater difficulties than young women in talking about their feelings and asking for help.

Young men are also more likely to be involved in drug or alcohol abuse and violence, and have better access to means of violent self-injury, such as firearms. When teenage boys do kill themselves, they are much more likely than girls to choose violent methods: to hang or shoot themselves, or slit their wrists.

Suicide figures also show big regional variations. In Scotland, youth suicide rates are much higher than they are in England and Wales, rising to 36 young men per 100,000. In Scotland and Northern Ireland, rates have increased dramatically in recent years. This seems to be linked to poor economic prospects, a lack of access to effective support, particularly in isolated rural communities, and sometimes to political issues.

What are the warning signs?

Because suicidal behaviour is complicated, so too are the warning signs. There's no single sign to look out for – it's more a case of being sensitive to the kinds of situations that make young people vulnerable. But there are some changes in behaviour that might suggest a teenager is feeling depressed and even suicidal. Someone may become increasingly aggressive or withdrawn, lose their appetite or stop interacting socially. They may dwell on negative thoughts or even begin to joke about suicide as a way of trying to articulate their pain.

The situation is made more complex by the fact that most checklists of warning signs include such 'normal' teenage behaviour as mood swings, inattentiveness in class and irregular attendance at school. Not every failure to hand in homework is a cry for help, but as a teacher you are well placed to recognize when a pupil's behaviour is out of the ordinary. Be aware, too, that suicide is more common in winter, particularly after Christmas.

So what can you do?

Dealing with suicide means treading a fine line between glamorizing it and failing to talk about it at all. The Samaritans recommend developing general programmes promoting good psychological and emotional health. These might also provide details of where young people can turn for help. If you suspect a young person may be suicidal then the main thing is to act quickly to get professional advice, from the pupil's GP, from a counselling organization or from mental health specialists.

Teenagers contemplating suicide may not know where to get help, so they turn to their teachers. But teachers are often wary of the additional responsibility, or frightened of acting wrongly. The main thing is to do something: while you might not be the ultimate solution you can act as first aid until professional help arrives. You may be the one person the child feels he or she can talk to. You're not being asked to be a counsellor, just to find a safe, private place to go and to take five minutes to get them the help they need. Experience shows that teenagers are likely to talk to a teacher on the spur of the moment, and if they don't get an immediate response they are unlikely to come back, while formal referrals can take months to process. In that time the person may be dead. Even if it seems like the worst possible timing, it may not be able to wait.

Don't presume that if someone who has been deemed a suicide 'risk' is prescribed anti-depressants then the problem is solved. Most health experts are wary about the value of drugs for children, and few would claim that drugs alone are enough to make a difference. Evidence suggests that you need a mixed approach, which includes helping teenagers find ways to solve their problems. This might include convincing them that their reactions are normal and setting them new goals to aim for. Just assuming suicidal young people must be psychologically ill is not always helpful – ask yourself how they might have got to that state and what might help them get through it. You may have just the personal knowledge needed to find the positives in their future which will keep them alive.

Talking the right language

Finding the right words to help a suicidal teenager is not easy. The Samaritans have tried a variety of ways to reach young people. They advertise on beer mats, have 'branches' in tents at rock festivals, and for ten years have been experimenting with an e-mail service, officially launched in 2002. They now receive around 300 e-mails a day from young people who are embarrassed to call helplines, or who feel their problems are not severe enough to warrant face-to-face advice. E-mail also helps people feel more in control: they can take time to write it and cope with the response.

While this kind of round-the-clock support is best left to the experts, there are measures which you can take in school which could be a big help. The training of peer mentors, for example, has proved a particularly successful initiative. Oxford University research has shown that 41 per cent of potential suicides turn to their friends first, but that most young people have no idea what to do if someone comes to them feeling suicidal. A peer mentor programme which trains students in listening skills and provides them with information about professional support can mean that desperate teenagers have someone to turn to at a critical time.

Suicide epidemics

Suicide is often described as 'contagious': in the school environment this can mean the problem just keeps getting bigger. Other pupils will often express open admiration for their dead friend's courage, for example, or crave the attention lavished on the person who has killed themselves. Nor does it necessarily have to be the suicide of a friend which has an impact – in January 2003 a 21-year-old in Phoenix, Arizona, took an overdose of prescription drugs while live on web-cam in front of an internet chatroom audience, who urged him on.

Acknowledging copycat behaviour can be particularly challenging. While the instinct may be to keep things quiet, the best thing to do is bring the powerful reactions to a suicide out into the open and allow others to express grief in their own way.

You're not alone...

Procedures for coping with bereavement at school may need to be changed after a suicide. There's still more stigma attached to death by suicide than by accident, and, depending on the school ethos, there may be moral or religious issues. It's also likely the local press will be camped outside the school gates, and there will be no shortage of spectators keen to apportion blame. Schools can be seen as a soft target. The first assumption is usually that the person must have been bullied and it's not easy to defend yourself against rumours. The police will also be involved.

If your school has a suicide prevention plan, then make sure you are familiar with it. If it doesn't, then it might be worth considering developing one (with a section on what to do if a suicide occurs): it means there are written guidelines which everyone can use as a basis for action. Most local authorities and community health professionals will be able to offer advice on putting something together. The Trust for the Study of Adolescence publishes a training pack with exercises for groups and advice on how to assess risk. And local branches of the Samaritans can organize school visits, with project material for use in the classroom, as well as offering help for staff.

Chapter 9
When you're sick

Each year 2.7 million teaching days are lost through sickness. In 2003–04 nearly 2,000 teachers took early retirement on grounds of ill health. A large secondary school with an average number of absences could face annual supply costs of up to £100,000. Nationally, the bill is around £300 million. Classes are disrupted, work programmes interrupted and remaining staff overburdened.

Are teachers in a worse state than other workers?

No. A 2002 survey by the Chartered Institute of Personnel and Development ranked education ninth in its league table of sickness, with teachers having fewer days off sick than policemen, health workers or civil servants. A teacher in the maintained sector has an average of 5.5 to 6.5 days off work each year because of illness, while those in independent schools take about five days. But the headline statistics don't tell the whole story. For example, DfES figures for 2002 show that 43 per cent of teachers didn't take a single day off due to illness, which means the average absence rate of the remaining 57 per cent was close to 10 days a year. And while comparisons with other public sector workers look good, teachers work a shorter year than most, so the proportion of days lost is higher. Nor do the statistics for time off reflect that as part of a 'caring profession', many teachers struggle into school when unwell, while others habitually suffer ill health when term finishes.

Long-term despair, short-term disruption

An alarming number of teachers are on long-term sick leave. Defined as an absence of more than 20 consecutive days, this accounts for 43 per cent of all teaching days lost to sickness and reflects the increasing number of teachers suffering serious ill health. It's also directly linked to the numbers who take early retirement on medical grounds. But while staff attendance rates can easily be affected by long-term sickness, it is the recurring bouts of tummy upsets and the sniffles that cause real problems. A succession of one or two-day absences can cause far more disruption than a six-month absence.

Why do teachers take time off work?

Teachers catch the same bugs as everyone else. As in most professions, the most common causes of absence in teaching are colds, flu and respiratory problems. Working with large numbers of children in small spaces doesn't help. The second most common cause is stomach trouble, the one category in which teaching outstrips other professions. On a happier note, teachers suffer fewer back problems than most workers.

What about stress?

Stress-related absence comes fourth down the list, behind migraines and headaches. But of all the statistics, this is the most misleading. In a survey of 350 headteachers, a majority said 'more than 50 per cent' of all their staff absences had stress as the root cause. Yet estimating the true impact of stress on health and well-being is impossible. There are well-established links, for example, between stress and stomach complaints or headaches – but even coughs and colds may be the result of an immune system being weakened by stress. Many doctors report that even though teachers turn up at surgery with physical symptoms, a bit more delving often uncovers stress as the real problem.

Stress-related illness can be a particular difficulty for headteachers, even if they seem to take few days off work. A 2000 study of 300 Warwickshire members of the National Association of Head Teachers found that one in three was on regular medication for stress, and one in four reported serious health problems including high blood pressure, chronic insomnia and eating disorders. Although their attendance and performance at school may have been as reliable as ever, the pressures were showing in other ways. More than half claimed their family lives had suffered, and one in six said they were alcoholics.

The feel-good factor

Just as hospital wards are being encouraged to take steps to get cleaner and healthier, so there are some basic measures which can make classrooms better places to be in. Some schools strongly discourage staff and pupils who are unwell from attending school, so they don't infect others but when it comes to controlling the spread of viruses and bacteria, just as in hospitals, promoting good basic hygiene is key. Washing your hands often is recognized as the best way of limiting the spread of bacteria, so making sure you have easy access to a basin makes sense. As does getting into the habit of using it. This may mean more than just washing your hands before tucking into your sandwich. It can be helpful to keep a note of the number of times you end up picking something off the floor or sharing pens, whiteboard markers, keyboards or a computer mouse. You might be surprised at how the opportunities for swapping germs add up. This can be particularly true at primary level, where snotty noses and grubby hands are more likely to come into the equation.

Believe it or not, tackling stress is easier than tackling germs. Stress is a set of symptoms, and these can be helped with medication or a change in lifestyle. The next step is getting to the root of the problem. This can be more tricky, but teachers should not be frightened of asking for help from senior colleagues. This might be a request for some professional advice: a report compiled in late 2001 for the Teachers Benevolent Fund (now the Teacher Support Network) concluded that workplace counselling could help cut staff sickness by reducing stress and highlighting problems before they escalate. Or it might be addressing the workload issue. Some schools have experimented with everything from a shortened school day to giving staff one free afternoon a week, in an attempt to reduce stress and sickness levels.

Other ways to keep in the pink of health include making sure you drink plenty of water throughout the day and using the school's sports facilities whenever you can. Some staffrooms even start the day with group t'ai chi or yoga. In the United States, however, a material approach is, literally, paying dividends. Staff absences have fallen drastically in Arlington, Texas, since the education authority gave schools a set budget for hiring supply teachers, with any unspent cash handed back to regular staff at the end of the year. The best attenders receive the most money.

Iron fist or helping hand?

There will always be teachers who find the lure of daytime TV an attractive alternative to Year 11 and *Lord of the Flies*. Every staff room has its malingerers and it's in your interest to support efforts to get tough. Getting teachers back in the classroom means less disruption (and more money) for the whole school.

But while some teachers aren't at work when they should be, others struggle on when they should take time off. 'Sometimes teachers need to listen to their bodies, rather than working until they break down,' says John Bangs, head of education at the National Union of Teachers. 'It's easy to feel that if you take time off the children will suffer, or you'll fall behind with the curriculum. But if you're in teaching for the long haul, you need to pace things and look after yourself.' If you notice a colleague is struggling with their health, a quiet word may help. But it's no good being a martyr yourself at the same time. If you feel you're reaching breaking point, then do something about it. Don't wait until you finally snap. While everyone has good days and bad days – even good weeks and bad weeks – you are in the best position to know if your health is genuinely suffering. Then it's time to get professional medical help and face up to the fact that you may have to have time off.

Getting insured

Private health insurance as a staff perk is probably beyond the means of most schools, but there are alternatives. Some mutual health organizations offer special deals to those working in the public sector. Schools can join for around £1 per teacher per week, giving staff access to free consultations with specialists and covering the cost of a wide range of treatments and surgery. You may feel uncomfortable suggesting your school signs up to this kind of scheme, but it's worth looking at the benefits and asking around to see whether colleagues like the idea. It's not only that schemes give you access to treatment more quickly than through the NHS – so cutting absence rates – but if a school chooses to invest in staff health it can be a real boost to morale.

Getting back to work

Even after only a few day's sick leave, you may face a 'back-to-work' interview on your return to the classroom. These can be uncomfortable – no-one likes reliving those miserable days in bed – but can be helpful too. Logging the exact details of your sickness helps schools trace a pattern, and presuming you are not trying to avoid certain classes on a regular basis, this may throw up particular problems caused by your environment. Do you often get throat or chest problems when you've been working in a certain building, for example? Could a better classroom chair help with that sore back? It's easy to feel threatened by managers interrogating you about your symptoms, but a routine 'back-to-work' interview can in fact give you the chance to raise concerns about working conditions.

If you're unlucky enough to be off sick for a long time, you might need more lengthy discussion with the school to work out a flexible plan for getting you back to work. It's worth considering easing yourself back in gently, perhaps by returning in an unofficial capacity for a short while to help as a classroom assistant, or by working part-time for a specified period. If you feel you need to take permanent account of the changes in your health, talk to your union which will be able to give advice on renegotiating job descriptions to accommodate the necessary adjustments.

Can the LEA help?

Most LEAs have occupational health nurses, but you are unlikely to get a routine appointment unless you have been off sick for some time. It may be worth pressing for one earlier, however, if you feel a medical professional with particular knowledge of life as a teacher could offer useful advice. Oxfordshire County Council, for example, has England's lowest proportion of teachers taking time off work. This is partly attributed to a policy of encouraging staff to visit occupational health specialists at an early stage. Not all teachers have this option, however. In several authorities, schools have to buy into the occupational health scheme from their own budget, and many choose not to do so.

On the other hand, some LEAs are taking positive steps. A handful have appointed 'well-being co-ordinators' as part of a scheme designed by Worklife Support, an offshoot of the Teacher Support Network. Their job is to carry out confidential questionnaires, asking staff about all aspects of school life, to build up a picture of the well-being of staff in the school and recommend changes. This can include seemingly trivial matters, such as a nicer staffroom or better toilets, all of which adds up to affect well-being and so, in turn, can cut sickness absence. The co-ordinators can also offer advice to individuals. This can include putting teachers in touch with practitioners offering alternative therapies such as massage or aromatherapy. Almost two-thirds of schools involved in the scheme report staff attendance as being 'much improved'.

Classic cars

Research by Dr Tony Bowers at the University of Cambridge into the causes and effects of teacher sickness revealed that teachers over 45 have substantially more time off work than younger staff. 'Teachers are like cars,' says Dr Bowers. 'The more miles on the clock, the more likely they are to break down.' The most reliable model, it seems, is the male teacher under 30, though from then on it's females who prove more roadworthy. And while there's a sharp drop in reliability after 45, there's actually an upturn when teachers reach their late fifties. 'We call it "the survivor effect",' says Dr Bowers. 'If teachers are still in the profession at that point, the chances are that they've found good strategies for avoiding illness, or that they're just naturally healthy people. If you want to find ways of avoiding absence, these are the people you should be talking to.'

Chapter 10
Teachers' sabbaticals

Feeling the blues? Fed up seeing the same grey faces in the staffroom? Then it's worth knowing there might be a chance to get a new life, or at least spruce up the old one, while doing something that could make a real difference to you and your school. Whether you fancy an exchange Down Under, a chance to don an Oxbridge gown or an insight into industry, somewhere out there is a scheme for you.

Am I entitled to anything?

Unfortunately not. The United Kingdom lags behind many other countries when it comes to offering teachers a well-earned change. In Australia, for example, you are entitled to a full year's sabbatical once every three years at 60 per cent of full pay, or every five years at 80 per cent salary. The downside is that you effectively finance these yourself by paying into a trust fund each year. A similar scheme operates in Canada, usually with a government top-up involved. Mainland Europe, too, has a greater degree of entitlement – in France, for example, ten years' teaching earns a term's sabbatical, albeit at your own expense. But while British teachers are short of rights, they aren't short of opportunities. When it comes to exchanges we tend to have an advantage over our European counterparts, simply because English is so widely spoken around the world.

The main difficulty is that there's a confusing hotchpotch of funds and funders, rather than a centrally administered series of schemes. While there are plenty of opportunities, it's a case of trawling through the small ads and keeping your ears to the ground.

What's the difference between a sabbatical, an exchange scheme, a research fellowship and a placement?

An exchange is a straightforward job swap. You will probably be expected to take on your exchange partner's full timetable, although you may be excused extra-curricular responsibilities. A sabbatical is a period of leave, usually granted as a reward for long service. Traditionally, someone receiving a sabbatical was free to spend the time as he or she wanted; nowadays strings tend to be attached. A research fellowship offers the chance to undertake a period of study under the guidance of a university. Some are full-time posts for up to a year, others allow you to continue with your job and put in the hours in your spare time. A placement, or secondment, typically involves spending a short period – up to six weeks – in industry or commerce. As well as learning about life in a non-school environment, the visiting teacher is expected to find ways of applying his or her classroom skills for the benefit of the company. Study visits last about a week and offer the chance to observe good practice in another school, usually overseas.

Exchange as good as a rest?

The idea of a teacher exchange is simple: you step into someone else's shoes, and they step into yours. The trick is in making sure you're the same shoe size. It can be the first few weeks – both going out and getting home – which are tough, but the key to a smooth ride lies in preparation. Take advantage of any induction meetings set up by the exchange body, and find out all you can about the education system and the syllabus you'll be teaching. Finding an appropriate exchange partner means thinking about everything from term dates to exchange rates. If you end up teaching a radically different syllabus, you may spend weekends cramming your subject instead of seeing the sights. Fortunately, there are several organizations to act as matchmaker and help with the practical details. But if you think you can swap your one-bedroom terrace for a sprawling Californian villa with its own pool, think again. The criteria for exchanges are geared towards making a seamless swap rather than bagging an exotic holiday, and it's usually about benefits for your school as much as topping up your tan.

With most exchange schemes you keep your own salary and continue to pay tax as if you were resident in the United Kingdom – so your pension won't be affected. Travel costs are usually covered by the organizing body, but not the travel costs of family members. Some schemes include insurance, others don't. Once you're out there it's up to you to manage your finances. There's a temptation to spend money like you're on holiday and some teachers run up big debts. Exchanging accommodation as well as jobs saves cash, but bills or repairs can be a problem. Don't be pressured into it if you're unsure. Swapping cars is almost always a disaster. Some people who do exchange house and car prefer to draw up a legal contract. And never agree to look after pets – witness the teacher who was landed with his exchange partner's two incontinent cats, which were later shot by a neighbour. A difficult phone-call.

Socially, you'll probably be seen as a bit of a novelty and get plenty of invitations, especially if you're single. But be prepared for some suspicious parents. One teacher who spent a year in a high school near Detroit, found that there were complaints to the principal: parents assumed that a teacher from England would stop work for elevenses and afternoon tea! Keep an open mind and a ready smile.

Once you opt for an exchange, you're stuck with it. But if the thought of a full year abroad has you reaching for your comfort blanket, think short term. It's possible to organize termly swaps to the United States, while European exchanges start from as little as three weeks.

Making a difference

The challenge of teaching classes of up to 120 children with few resources and a long walk home to a local dwelling is something a lot of teachers think about – then dismiss. But your teaching skills are nowhere more valuable, or valued, than in the developing world. VSO now offers one-year placements for primary teachers, and an education managers programme, aimed at headteachers, which also has one-year opportunities. These shorter placements should ease negotiations on a sabbatical arrangement, so you can return to your old job after a spell abroad. Some teachers, especially those in faith schools, have even negotiated leave of absence for standard two-year placements, emphasizing to their governing bodies the personal and professional development opportunities as well as the obvious contribution to less wealthy education systems.

Just give me a break!

God only had to work six days for his first sabbatical; you'll probably have to put in at least ten years. The word 'sabbatical' refers to anything connected with the Sabbath, or day of rest. It was in the 1800s that the word took on its more secular meaning of a period of leave earned by long service. Sadly, the days when sabbaticals offered a complete break from the day job have largely disappeared; most grants nowadays come with work-related strings attached. But there is a glorious exception. The Goldsmiths' Company's mid-career refreshment grant is specifically for projects with no obvious link to the classroom. 'Originality, combined with passion and determination to pursue a long-harboured ambition, are the keys to getting a grant,' says Goldsmiths'. Recently, grants have been awarded to teachers to study Maori culture in New Zealand, lead a string quartet in Sweden and trace a grandparent's footsteps across Kansas.

The Goldsmiths' grants are to reward long service and to recharge the batteries for the final push to retirement. Some independent schools offer similar opportunities. At Eton college, for example, teachers are given a full paid term on sabbatical after ten years. Teachers propose their own projects with the key being 'refreshment'.

Doing the business

Placements in business and industry are popular with teachers who hanker after a taste of the outside world. Heads, Teachers and Industry (HTI) organizes around 50 business placements a year, lasting between six weeks and a year. Teachers are linked to businesses who need specific skills for short-term projects. The benefits are mutual. The business gets a specialist consultant at a reasonable price, while the secondee gets the opportunity for first-hand management experience.

Jolly good fellowships

Ever struggled to find the book you want, or somewhere quiet to work? Then swapping the mayhem of the school corridor for the cloistered calm of an Oxbridge quadrangle may give you the facilities and breathing space you need. With an emphasis on personal academic research, Oxford and Cambridge schoolteacher fellowships typically come with no teaching responsibilities, just accommodation, food and a free run of the libraries. Teachers who have been awarded a fellowship report being given outstanding sets of rooms and full dining rights as well as access to the wine cellar.

But it's not all grouse and claret. The fellowships are intended for those who teach the 16–18 age group, and the idea is to break down preconceptions and encourage applications from the maintained sector.

Schoolteacher fellows are expected to meet admissions tutors from a variety of colleges, and explore issues of access and widening participation.

Most colleges offer some kind of placement, but there's no centralized process for applying. If it's something you fancy, it's worth ringing round admissions offices. The scheme isn't widely known and some colleges struggle to fill places.

What's the first step?

All the organizations have their own forms and procedures. If you're interested in a scheme, you'll need to make contact to find out the deadline for applications. And remember that before applying for an exchange, sabbatical or research fellowship, you must have the support of your headteacher. Some heads have been known to reject requests out of hand. More likely they will want to discuss the timing of your absence. Even if the school receives a teacher in exchange, or funds to cover the cost of supply, disruption is inevitable. Some heads say recruitment problems and the move towards modular exams have made it difficult to approve long periods out of school. If you have something major in mind, like a one-year exchange, it's probably worth mooting the idea at least 12 months before you apply. If you give the school enough warning and make a convincing case for professional benefits, you might be pleasantly surprised.

Do I have to write a report when I get back?

At least one – probably more. You could be looking at up to 5,000 words. Some schemes insist on a first report within a few weeks of arriving back, and a follow-up a few months later to show how you've integrated your new-found wisdom into school life. You may well find yourself published on the internet, and be prepared for the occasional PR request: charming the benefactors over canapes, chatting to inquisitive journalists or putting on a slide show for potential applicants are all part of the deal.

In practice

The Goldmiths' mid-career refreshment break gave me the chance to be a bit selfish and do something I would never usually take the time to do. For three years in succession, I cut out the advertisement, intending to apply but, as usual, school work took over and I never quite got round to it. But 2002 was different. My daughter sat me down, and made sure that, despite having the school play to produce, reports to write and impending school inspections, I completed and posted the application.

Since reading the novels of Jack London as a child, I've had an enduring fascination with the Klondike gold rush of 1897, and over the years, have read about the exploits of the stampeders who made the journey north to the Yukon with dreams of striking it rich. I was particularly interested in the contribution women made and, for years, I'd hoped to travel there for myself and find out more about the part they played. The application process was easy and Goldsmiths' made the selection straightforward; it wasn't daunting and I felt they were personally interested in what I was doing. I was thrilled when my project was accepted. I spent evenings after school in fitness training in the hills around my home in Northumberland, contacting museums and libraries where I would concentrate my research, and preparing resources for the supply teacher who would take over from me. Then, in summer 2003, I was off. I had a month. I flew to Seattle, the start of the Klondike trail, then made my way up the northwest coast by boat to Skagway, Alaska. From there I hiked over the coastal mountains and followed the stampeders' trail to Whitehorse and on to Dawson City and the gold fields, a journey of about 2,000 miles.

Tourists often go to Dawson City, but they don't usually go over the mountains. Only a certain number of people are allowed on the historic trail each year, so I had to apply in advance for a pass from the national park. I wanted to trace the experiences of English women there in the 1890s. I talked to many of their descendants who still live there and discovered the tragic implications of the gold rush on the Native Americans, the impact of which is still unhappily visible. I searched through mountains of archive information in local libraries, and the letters and diaries opened a fascinating window on these women, who challenged the Victorian conventions of the day with their spirit of independence and adventure.

One of the highlights was canoeing along the Teslin and Yukon rivers, following in the path of women from the Victorian Order of Nurses who made the trip to Dawson in 1898 to look after typhoid victims. I spent heady days paddling through this vast wilderness: the silence and immense feeling of solitude as I passed skeletal hulks of sternwheelers that had plied these once busy waters, their derelict cabins fast disappearing into the undergrowth, gave a sense of history that was almost tangible. I hadn't travelled on my own for years. It felt odd for the first few days; then it was fantastic. Staying in hostels, I wasn't treated like a middle-aged lady but like any of the young travellers. It did my self-esteem a lot of good.

Although the break had nothing to do with my teaching, it did make a difference when I got back to school. Not only was I refreshed and enthusiastic, but the children could see it was possible to do something adventurous; it led to a pupil here going off on an adventure trip to New Zealand. Few people get the chance to indulge themselves in a passion like this. It offered me the opportunity of a lifetime and I would encourage anyone to apply. The rewards are tremendous.

Gillian Dalby teaches English and Drama at Nunnykirk Centre for Dyslexia, Northumberland.

Part II

The thinking classroom

The last decade has seen a resurgence of interest in the art of teaching. Buzz-words such as learning styles, thinking skills and emotional intelligence have been conjured out of corporate training days and government white papers. Often it's old ideas, dusted down, spruced up, and given a new lease of life. Other times it's new concepts born out of scientific or technological advances.

In all cases, it's a lot of information to take in. Many of these developments have been conceived, not in schools themselves, but in government offices. They reach teachers as a restrictive one-size-fits-all package, or as a well-meaning but vague series of directives. The challenge for teachers is to find a way through the rhetoric and jargon; to blend new ideas with their own tried and tested practice.

But however off-putting the packaging may be, most of us would agree that teaching children to think clearly and creatively is one of the best things we can do. It's a common mantra that schools are not just about exam results but about preparing children for life. Education in the early twenty-first century is in state of flux. Since learning to use an internet search engine now effectively means all the facts you may ever need are at your fingertips for life, employers are increasingly rewarding originality and adaptability. The emphasis is on skills, rather than knowledge.

But a combination of league table pressure, ingrained habits, lurking Ofsted inspectors and it-wasn't-like-that-in-my-day parents means it's not always easy to change the way you work. Exploring some of the subjects covered in this section may be one way forward.

Chapter 11
Using questions

Teachers ask up to two questions every minute, up to 400 in a day, around 70,000 a year, or two to three million over the course of a career. Clearly, questioning is an integral part of the teaching process. So it's worth making sure you ask the right ones in the right way.

Why do teachers ask so many questions?

When Socrates defined teaching as 'the art of asking questions', he had in mind the cut and thrust of lofty philosophical debate. The prosaic truth of the modern-day classroom is rather different. Four hundred questions a day may seem a startling statistic, but a large proportion of these (anything between 30 and 60 per cent) are procedural rather than learning-based. In other words, they tend to be of the is-your-name-on-it? or have-you-finished-yet? variety.

But questioning is still a key means of knowledge transfer. It accounts for up to a third of all teaching time, second only to the time devoted to explanation. And many experts believe it should be even more prominent. The consensus is that good learning starts with questions not answers, and that teachers who develop their questioning skills can deliver more enjoyable and interactive lessons to their students.

Questions serve many purposes. They can help pupils to reflect on information and commit it to memory. They can develop thinking skills, encourage discussion and stimulate new ideas. Questions allow teachers to determine how much a class understands and enable them to pitch lessons at an appropriate level. They are an important tool for managing the classroom, helping to draw individuals into the lesson and keeping them interested and alert. And questions have a symbolic value – sending a clear message that pupils are expected to be active participants in the learning process.

What is a question?

Learning to recognize various types of questions – and the functions they serve – is one of the keys to effective questioning. Different experts categorize questions in different ways. The late Ted Wragg, emeritus professor of education at Ereter University, offered a model comprising three groups: empirical (requiring answers based on facts); conceptual (concerned with definitions and reasoning); and value questions (investigating personal beliefs and moral issues). The DfES talks of product questions (which work towards an answer), and process questions (which focus on the method or reasoning). Bloom's Taxonomy of Learning, Teaching and Assessing, on the other hand, categorizes questions according to whether they test knowledge, comprehension, analysis, application, synthesis or evaluation.

But the simplest and most important distinction, recognized by all experts, is between lower-order questions, which require children to remember, and higher-order questions, which require them to think. As a general rule, lower-order or factual recall questions tend to be closed, with a single right answer, and are likely to be what, who, when or where. Higher-order are more likely to start with how, why or which, and tend to be open – with a range of possible responses.

Which questions should I be asking?

Factual recall questions can be a useful teaching tool. They keep the lesson moving, they reassure you that knowledge is being passed on and allow you to check that no-one is getting left behind. If questions are being asked and answered correctly, it creates an atmosphere of achievement and progress. But most research suggests teachers ask too many of these basic recall questions and not enough thought-provoking, higher-order questions. A 1989 study of secondary school lessons by Lincoln University's Professor Trevor Kerry found that only 4 per cent of questions were of a higher-order nature. And Ted Wragg's 1994 research in primary schools produced similar results – only 8 per cent of questions were of a higher-order nature.

For many teachers it seems that a particular style of questioning becomes habitual. Lower-order questioning is easy, familiar and almost addictive. The danger is that pupils who don't know the answers can feel like failures. The classroom becomes a place of testing not learning, the teacher is reduced to the role of quiz-show host, rather than educator.

A report by US educationist Kathleen Cotton in 1988, which examined 37 research projects to do with questioning across the United States, came to two important conclusions. First, that at all ages, a combination of higher-order and lower-order questions was the most effective method. And second, that with pupils of top primary or secondary school ages, increasing the proportion of higher-order questions to around 50 per cent brought significant gains in terms of student attitude and performance.

Your time starts now...

Life after death? The chicken or the egg? The sound of one hand clapping? Some questions preoccupy philosophers for a lifetime or span centuries of civilization. Most questions asked in the classroom are answered in less than a second. That's the average time teachers allow between posing a question and accepting an answer, throwing the question to someone else or even answering it themselves. Weaker pupils are often given even less time – usually because the teacher is afraid of embarrassing them, or lacks confidence in their coming up with the right answer.

But another US study, conducted in New York in 1978 by Mary Budd Rowe, found that increasing the 'wait time' improved the number and quality of the responses. For a lower-order recall question, three seconds was found to be the optimum wait time, while more than 10 seconds produced even better results with higher-order questions. The same research also found that extending the wait time between the pupil giving the answer and the teacher commenting on it (typically fractions of a second) allows pupils to revise or expand their response, and encourages other pupils to contribute.

Sometimes, having the self-discipline to remain silent is all that's needed to draw out more thoughtful responses. Moving away from rapid-fire questioning also encourages children to take their time. And to really get the class thinking, try finishing the lesson with a question which pupils can ponder over for discussion the following day.

To question or not to question?

Not all children like to be asked questions. Shyness, lack of confidence, or bad experiences with previous teachers can all cause some children to fear being singled out. Some children even admit to choosing to sit in the part of the classroom where they feel they are least likely to be asked a direct question by the teacher.

Part of the problem is that questions aren't just a learning tool. As MPs, barristers, policemen and journalists all know, they can be used to manipulate or accuse. Lower-order questions, in particular, are often closely linked to behaviour management, with teachers using them as a means of control in the classroom. It's a common tactic to fire-off questions like disciplinary bullets at children who aren't paying attention – and it can be tempting to ask ones they won't be able to answer, just to prove their whispered conversation at the back of the classroom really is a barrier to learning.

Even when questions aren't being used as part of a power struggle, pupils can still find interrogation intimidating. Often, a child's main fear is not of being wrong, but of looking silly – saying something that will be ridiculed by the teacher or other pupils. Such 'peer fear' is the main obstacle to children answering and asking questions. Asking easier questions to weaker pupils in the hope they'll get something right doesn't seem to be the answer, as they increase the fear of being wrong. In fact, many children are most happy to venture their opinions when they believe no one else in the class knows the answers.

Effective questioning – who to ask?

Reserving your questions for those pupils who are most likely to know the answer is a good way of ensuring a quick-moving lesson, but a poor way of developing thinking skills. Getting your questions to produce some kind of response in every pupil – even if it is a covert response that is never voiced aloud – is the knack to clever questioning. A hands-up approach where children volunteer answers can lead to a few pupils dominating the lesson. Putting a question to the whole class, then asking an individual to respond – sometimes called the 'pose, pause and pounce' technique – allows you to target questions at specific children, but research suggests the lesson is still likely to centre around six to eight main contributors, who are usually in the teacher's immediate line of vision.

A better approach may be to move away altogether from the idea of targeting individuals, and focus instead on getting the class to work together to tease out the answers to challenging questions. With this kind of collective questioning, pupils aren't being asked to provide an answer, they are simply being invited to make a contribution. The teacher takes on the role of a mentor coaxing out answers, and helping out when the ideas run dry. Creating a comfortable environment where being right doesn't always matter will help ensure that it isn't always the quickest and most confident pupils who make those contributions.

Getting children to ask questions

At the age of five, children ask dozens of questions a day – many of them higher-order questions starting with 'why'. But they don't ask questions in school. Ted Wragg's 1993 research found that an average of just one spontaneous question each lesson came from the pupils, and that was more likely to do with procedure than with learning. Effective questioning isn't a one-way process. If you are asking the kind of questions that stimulate thought and debate, there's a strong chance your pupils will start to fire some questions back at you.

There are plenty of strategies for encouraging children to ask more questions. Holding back on a new topic until the class has worked out what questions they would like answered in the course of the following lessons can get the curiosity juices flowing. And asking pupils to set tests at the end of a topic for other children in the class – awarding marks for the quality of the questions rather than the quality of the answers – can get them used to the varied forms of possible questions.

They need to know that questions aren't as scary as they might seem; using search engines on the internet to pose inquiries, working in small groups or making a question wall where students and teachers can pin up questions they would like answering, can all help overcome the natural fear of being caught out not knowing.

Above all, questions should be seen to be important. Finishing a lesson on the stroke of the bell with the familiar call of 'Any questions?' (which, of course, really means 'There aren't any questions, are there?') sends out the message that questions are a nuisance. It's worth making room with designated question time lessons, or asking children to come back for the next lesson with a question to ask. This will make it clear that they are encouraged and valued.

It ain't what you ask, it's the way that you ask it...

One of the main reasons children fail to respond is a failure to understand the question itself. Pitching questions in a manner the whole class finds easy to understand is common sense, but not always easy to achieve when you're thinking on your feet. If the question you ask doesn't get much of a response, try rephrasing rather than repeating. And try to present questions as part of a sequence which makes them seem clearly and logically connected. Most of the questions teachers ask arise spontaneously during the course of a lesson, but it may be worth having one or two pre-planned questions, perhaps written on the board, around which each lesson can be structured.

And it's not just a matter of what you ask, or how – but also of when you ask it. Lower-ability and younger children may respond more effectively to questions presented after they have been given the opportunity to look at material. With higher-ability children it's the other way round – asking questions before they have seen the material allows them to examine it with particular inquiries in mind, and elicits better responses.

Having the answers

How you deal with the responses to your questions might shape a whole lesson. It's important to show an interest in a reply rather than just moving on or correcting it. It may well slow down, or even hijack, the best-planned lesson, but be prepared to digress. Good replies will always raise further questions, and if children feel their responses aren't being valued then they will soon stop contributing.

Whatever line of questioning you choose, whatever techniques you adopt, be prepared to do some analysis of how you work. The questioning process is largely instinctive – with only a split second's thought before deciding what to ask, who to ask, and how to ask it. Videoing your own lessons may be the only way to study the type of questioning that takes place and to establish what's working and what isn't.

Chapter 12
Handwriting

Everyone's handwriting is unique – a reflection of individual mood and personality. But if you met up with the children who shared your primary classroom, you'd probably find that one of the few things you still had in common would be the way you loop your 'g's and cross your 't's. There's plenty of debate about the best way to teach handwriting, and about the style of writing that should be taught. Italic or round hand? Slanting or straight? In some countries there's no choice, teachers have to follow a prescribed national style. In the United Kingdom, the decision rests with individual schools.

A brief history...

Most present-day styles of handwriting have their roots in Italian styles of the sixteenth century, popularised in England in 1570 by the publication of the first 'writing manual'. At that time, reading and writing were separate skills and only lawyers, doctors, businessmen, clergymen and clerks were taught to write. For the next 200 years different styles of handwriting were learned by different social groups. The legal profession, for example, adopted an elaborate style, while the world of commerce used a simpler, clearer hand. Early Victorians used a copperplate style with thick and thin strokes, but later in the nineteenth century, the less fussy 'Vere Foster civil service' hand, named after the Irishman who invented it, became the most frequently taught model in schools. It remained popular into the twentieth century, though it had to compete with a revival in italics and a movement towards 'print-script' – simplified letters that reflected the growing use of typewriters. But its eventual successor was the semi-cursive, or 'joined-up' style known as 'round hand', developed in the 1930s. Most schools now teach a derivative of this.

Laying it on the line?

Some countries, such as France and the United States, have traditionally encouraged national styles of handwriting, though guidelines have been relaxed recently. It guarantees children an element of continuity. The United Kingdom, on the other hand, has a long tradition of handwriting diversity, and the only government guidance is that the style first taught should be 'easy to join later'. This has encouraged a proliferation of handwriting schemes and schools can face some bewildering choices. Italic styles carry an air of sophistication, but aren't generally suited to fast writing. A fully cursive style, in which all letters are joined, is usually quicker, but can look over-elaborate with loopy 'g's and 'y's. Currently, the most commonly taught style is semi-cursive, but choices remain between round or oval letters, straight or slanting – and that's before considering individual letter options such as round or pointed 'w's.

In the absence of government guidelines, most schools try to encourage a consistent approach – even to the extent of asking teachers to always use the same style when they write on the board, or produce displays and notices.

Or going with the flow?

A school model can be helpful, but enforcing it in a draconian way is not. Some children tend towards an individual style from the start, with a natural flow of the hand that lends itself to a rounded or italic style. In any case, handwriting is a way of expressing our personality, and even children who start out by following a rigid model soon develop their idiosyncrasies. But teachers have an important role to play in checking that younger children are following a style that is comfortable, legible and potentially fast. It can be very hard to change styles once habits have been formed – so whilst it's good to allow individuality, it's also important to make sure there's nothing that will disadvantage a child in later years.

So what's so complicated?

Everyone agrees that letter formation, spacing and direction are the fundamental principles children must learn. But opinions vary as to the best way of teaching these skills. Some favour a visual approach, with children learning to copy by close attention to detail. Others lean towards cognitive methods, explaining handwriting as a code, or a series of conventions, which needs to be memorised. And some stress a kinaesthetic approach, with an emphasis on developing motor skills and practising patterns of movement. Almost all teachers, knowingly or unknowingly, will draw on all three strategies.

Not surprisingly, many teachers are daunted by the technicalities of teaching handwriting. A preliminary study of primary schools carried out by a team from the school of psychology and human development at the Institute of Education found only around one primary teacher in three had received instruction in teaching handwriting during initial teacher training. And while handwriting is now covered by the national literacy strategy (initially it was overlooked), there is still nothing like the wealth of material linked to reading.

Joined-up writing

The national literacy strategy suggests most children should be using 'legible, joined handwriting' by the end of Year 4. But the approach in the early years varies. Some schools say print script (separate letters) is easier for young children. But a growing number teach joined-up writing from the start, arguing that there is little point learning a skill only to unlearn it later on. But the debate about when and how to join is less important than the teaching of letter formation. If children start and end letters in the correct places, with appropriate exit strokes, joining simply becomes a matter of keeping the pen on the page between letters, rather than lifting it off.

But why should children be encouraged to join up, other than to stop their writing looking childish? Most experts insist a joined-up style is faster, although the research is far from conclusive; many children achieve impressive speeds while joining few if any of their letters.

Get a grip

Learning to hold a pen is the first step towards learning to write. The conventional grip is the 'dynamic tripod': the pen held between the pad of the thumb and index finger, and rested on the middle finger. But most children learn how to hold crayons before starting school, so may arrive with an unorthodox grip. This probably won't hinder them in the early stages, but there's a chance it will cause problems later on: 40 per cent of girls and 25 per cent of boys of school leaving age complain of suffering pain when writing quickly. Most secondary teachers will be all too familiar with the sight of tired exam candidates flexing their arms and shaking their hands.

Not that the dynamic tripod is a sure-fire answer. It was designed for ink pens, which few children use any more. The modern range of writing implements means no one grip covers all the options. A ball-point, for example, works best at a different angle to a rollerball or a fibre-tip. Should children choose a grip to suit their pen, or a pen to suit their grip? And the grip is just one part of the handwriting posture – the positions of the head, arm and wrist are also important. For teachers, the important thing is to find ways to help individuals, which means watching how children write, as they write, not just looking at finished work.

A write way to spell?

Some experts argue that teaching spelling and handwriting together has a positive effect, as children find it easier to remember spellings if they can remember the movement of the hand in forming the word; hence the reason most people, when asked to spell a difficult word, prefer to write it down. Children with dyslexia may find this kind of multi-sensory approach particularly helpful when learning new spellings.

Left out in the cold

Left-handers make up around 15 per cent of the population, and learning to write presents them with particular challenges. At one time, many schools forced left-handed children to become right-handed, to avoid smudging as their hands moved across the page. Smudge-free pens have solved that problem and there are now pens designed specifically for left-handers. But they still face other difficulties. They may be short of elbow room if seated next to a right-hander, causing them to slant the paper or adopt a twisted posture to get a better view of what they're writing. And the left to right direction of English writing tends to be most comfortable for right-handed people. At least left-handers in the United Kingdom do not have to conform to a national model, and an understanding teacher who makes appropriate allowances will be able to prevent most potential problems.

Faster! Faster!

Is handwriting an art form, or merely a tool? Historically, schools have put the emphasis on neatness, rather than speed. Yet our exam system clearly suits children who can write quickly under pressure.

One possible approach is to encourage children to develop a 'fast-hand' for note-taking, and a 'best-hand' for more formal writing. But perhaps most important is developing a hand that is easily legible, yet fast enough to meet the demands of an exam room. Not only are quicker writers able to get more words down on paper, it may also be that an easy and fluent writing style helps improve the quality of what they write, by allowing them to concentrate more on the task in hand. A 1998 study, 'The Role of Handwriting in Raising Achievement', carried out by a research team at Lord Williams's school in Thame, Oxfordshire, found a clear link between handwriting speed and exam success. For example, girls who didn't join their letters performed a grade worse in English GCSE than those deemed to have similar academic ability, but with a more fluent writing style.

How fast?

Some children eventually achieve speeds of up to 40 words a minute, though research carried out for the DfES in 2001 by Penny Allcock found that Year 11 students manage an average of just under 17 words a minute. Exam board guidance indicates that children who write fewer than 12.7 words a minute may be eligible for extra time in exams, while those who average fewer than 10 can request permission to dictate their answers to a scribe.

Getting children to write quickly is largely a matter of ironing out technical problems and then practising, perhaps against the clock. But ongoing research at the Institute of Education suggests only around one in five primaries has an active approach to speeding up pupils' writing. A little-known bonus of learning to write quickly is that it may protect you against fraud: forensic handwriting experts claim that quickly produced writing is much more difficult to forge than slowly written script.

Neater! Neater!

In the exam room, speed may be of the essence, but beautiful handwriting has been valued since the Middle Ages, a tradition that continues. Many primary teachers report parents being particularly anxious for their children to have neat writing – sometimes it almost seems to matter more than whether they are actually learning anything.

But tidy writing does have benefits in the classroom. Because handwriting is essentially a motor skill, those whose other literacy skills are less developed can still produce work which at least looks good. And that may be enough to boost their self-esteem, and make them feel positive about their work.

Giving pens the push?

Over the next few years the spread of affordable, easily portable word-processing systems will mean most of us using paper and pen less frequently. But handwriting is likely to remain a necessary skill: handwritten exams, for example, are far easier to administer and invigilate. In the long-term, the biggest threat to the survival of handwriting – and typing – may be the development of voice-recognition technology, with computers turning speech into text. But there will probably always be situations in which putting pen to paper remains the quickest, easiest and cheapest form of communication.

Far from worrying about the future of handwriting, perhaps we should be lamenting instead a failure to teach keyboard skills. In the United States and Australia, schools promote touch-typing at a young age but in the United Kingdom this is still seen largely as a secretarial skill. In reality, of course, anyone using a computer benefits from being able to type quickly.

Joined-up thinking

Your school may already have a clear policy on handwriting. If so, it's important to communicate this to parents, and even prospective parents. Eager mums and dads often start children writing at home, which can lead to the formation of bad habits even before a child gets to school. Secondary teachers need to have a strategy for dealing with children arriving from several schools, each teaching a different model and it's worth being aware that children who arrive from a foreign culture may face specific difficulties. Arabic writing, for example, goes from right to left, so children may have to learn a whole new direction in their writing.

A handwriting policy should also address issues such as the type of paper used. How large will each sheet be? Will it be plain, squared, or lined – and will it have sets of lines to help place ascenders and descenders? It's important, too, to have a range of desk sizes, so everyone can be in a comfortable writing position. And it's not just primaries that need to give consideration to a handwriting policy: many pupils arrive at secondary school struggling to write quickly and neatly. Who will help them improve: the English department? A special needs teacher? Or the whole staff working across the curriculum?

A window on the soul?

Some companies employ graphologists to write character assessments of prospective employees, though most insist this is just a tiny part of the selection procedure. A quick glance at the *TES* jobs pages reveals that many schools, particularly independents, still like teachers to submit a handwritten letter of application. There are even self-help books on the market that claim changing your handwriting can be the first step to a more dynamic and successful life. Clearly, to a greater or lesser extent, our handwriting is a reflection of our self. Taking an interest in the handwriting of the children you teach may give you an early indication not only of potential learning difficulties, but also of emotional problems.

In practice

Children at Oldfield primary start to learn to write as soon as they arrive at school, but not by picking up a pencil or trying to form letters. Instead we work on patterning, which means getting their body used to making the fine motor movements they'll need later on. Our reception class uses shaving foam on the desks or chalk in the playground to practise writing zig-zags or curved shapes, usually with big arm movements. As their motor skills become finer, they can reduce the size of the shapes. It all means that, right from the start, the children associate handwriting lessons with having fun.

In Year 1 we teach the letters in groups, starting with straight ones (i, l, t and u), then the tunnel letters (h, m, n, b, p). By the end of Year 1, they will have been introduced to the formation of all the letters in the alphabet. We teach a form of fully cursive writing, in which all the letters will join up. Our dyslexic children find it easier. They can remember words as a single movement, instead of a broken series of separate movements. That helps with their writing and their spelling. We have dedicated handwriting lessons but the children also practise writing when they work on their spellings. And we reinforce the work on patterning by encouraging children to put a border around all the work they do, made of letter patterns such as continuous 'n's or 'v's. We teach the children that each letter starts and ends on the line, and that all letters have an entry stroke and an exit stroke. We get children to work with combinations of letters that form words, and, naturally, they start to join the letters. We don't tell them to, but they do it anyway. By the end of Year 2 most of the class will be writing continuous cursive.

Once the children are working well in pencil, we encourage them to experiment with a range of pens to find the one that suits them best. Favourites include the Berol handwriting pen, the Lamy fountain pen, and the Yoropen, which is oddly shaped but has finger grips to ensure a correct hold. That seems to suit some of the left-handers. There's also a Stabilo pen that comes in left and right-hand versions. We use traditional handwriting paper, with tramlines indicating where the main body of the letter should go and how far ascenders and descenders should extend. We have the paper in four sizes, again to allow children to start big, then gradually reduce the size of their writing when they're ready. Some children, especially left-handers, find it difficult to write on a flat desk, so we have writing slopes to put on the desk.

Our previous head introduced continuous cursive writing, initially to help dyslexic children. We soon found that what worked for them worked just as well for the others, including those with motor difficulties, and it has evolved from there. Developing neat handwriting can give children a real lift, especially when they see their work on the wall.

Bad habits are difficult to lose, so we prefer children to arrive with no experience of trying to write at nursery. I have two children who learned to write here at Oldfield, who are now at secondary school and going through the process of individualizing their writing. It bears little resemblance to what they learned here, but they still have the basics right, such as the correct grip. If you can teach children a good technique, it will stay with them for life.

Bonnie Walter is a learning support assistant at Oldfield Primary, Berkshire.

Chapter 13
Emotional intelligence

Touchy-feely mumbo-jumbo or a revolution in our schools? Common sense or neuroscience? On the simplest level, emotional intelligence (EI) is the ability to understand and talk about your emotions and those of other people. Emotional intelligence practitioners believe it can boost health and happiness, tackle challenging behaviour and improve academic performance. Critics suggest it's a fad. So, is EI anything more than another American buzz-word?

A brief history

The term was first coined in the United States in 1995 by psychologists John Mayer and Peter Salovey, who defined it as the ability to perceive, access, generate and reflectively regulate emotions so as to promote emotional and intellectual growth. The idea took off almost immediately when the American author and psychologist Daniel Goleman published his best-selling book, *Emotional Intelligence: Why It Can Matter More Than IQ (1995)*, which soon earned a cult following. By the late 1990s, many psychotherapists were using EI techniques and there was a mushrooming of corporate training aimed at getting employees in touch with their emotions.

The first EI initiative in the United Kingdom was launched by Southampton in 1997, looking first at anger management, then at social skills and self-esteem, and working with everyone from governors to lunchtime supervisors. Soon, schools nationwide were integrating aspects of EI into the curriculum and, in 2003, the DfES launched the Social, Emotional and Behavioural Skills (Sebs) pilot in 250 primary schools. The curriculum material developed as a result of that initiative was distributed to all primaries in 2005.

The fab five

Whilst interest in EI has spread widely and swiftly, not all schools or LEAs use the same terminology. Some prefer the phrase 'emotional literacy', and there are other banners, including 'emotional health and well-being' and 'emotional and social competence'. But whatever the name, the basic idea is the same: to encourage people's awareness of their feelings and ability to manage them.

Professor Goleman identified five key areas of EI. He defined 'self-awareness' as the capacity to recognize your feelings as they happen; 'emotional control' as the ability to manage your emotional reactions, control your impulses and recover from life's upsets; 'self-motivation' as the ability to use the emotions to pursue a goal, staying hopeful even in the face of setbacks; and 'empathy' as emotional sensitivity to other people's feelings; the fifth area was 'handling relationships', which encompasses social skills such as leadership, teamwork and confidence in dealing with other people.

The DfES strategy is based on a similar five skills: self-awareness, managing emotions, empathy, motivation and communication. For practitioners, the important aspect is not so much the definitions as making EI an equal partner with skills such as literacy and numeracy. Their view is that developing EI is not an optional extra which schools can take or leave, but rather a central part of the whole learning process.

The science bit

Most EI projects are a combination of common sense and cutting-edge neuroscience. Research has centred on the role of the prefrontal cortex, the part of the brain just behind the forehead, which develops most rapidly between the ages of 3 and 8. This acts as a kind of 'sensible parent', mediating our emotional impulses. These tend to come from the amygdala, an alarm tripwire that directs some of our most powerful and primitive feelings, such as fear, straight to all the major centres of the brain. The amygdala often cuts in before the neocortex – the site of more rational reactions – has had a chance to register what's going on. The job of the prefrontal cortex is to manage some of these instinctive emotions, dampening some of the signals generated by the amygdala and weighing up appropriate reactions.

Several LEAs in Wales, including Flintshire, Conwy, Denbighshire and Rhondda, use 'Paths' (promoting alternative thinking strategies), a scheme developed in the United States by Mark Greenberg, director of the prevention research centre at Penn State University in Philadelphia, and an expert on the prefrontal cortex. The Paths scheme takes as its starting point the belief that the prefrontal cortex has developed as a way of bringing together emotion, reason and cognition to ensure the evolutionary success of human beings.

Why is EI important?

Advocates of EI claim that people who are emotionally literate are more successful in their personal lives and their careers than those who are not. They believe that growing up in an emotionally literate atmosphere means children will tolerate frustration better, be less likely to self harm, be less lonely, less impulsive, more focused and healthier than others, and that they will achieve more academically. They believe EI affects health, education, behaviour and relationships; in short, it is the key to a successful lifestyle.

But does it work?

In 2002, the DfES commissioned Southampton University's health education unit to look at all the literature about EI as well as the work of several LEAs that were already committed to EI projects. Overall, the researchers found that schools developing programmes which fostered the emotional health of staff and pupils showed marked improvements in behaviour and learning, social cohesion, staff morale and confidence and academic results.

At Shacklewell primary school in the London borough of Hackney, deputy head Prue Barnes and colleague Justine Sampher won a DfES sabbatical to the United States to research EI projects, and, on their return, began to implement EI initiatives across the curriculum. The school has seen attendance figures and Sats results improve, and, in partnership with children's welfare charity, the National Society for the Prevention of Cruelty to Children (NSPCC), has launched a series of emotional intelligence classes for parents and carers which have the highest local take-up of any adult classes. 'But the biggest measure of success is that the children are in school and feel positively about being here,' says Ms Barnes. 'They can see that we take emotional health as seriously as physical well-being.'

What about IQ?

Intellectual intelligence does not necessarily make someone emotionally intelligent. Since publication in 1983 of the influential book *Frames of Mind* by Howard Gardner of Harvard School of Education, which identified the concept of 'multiple intelligences', much research has focused on the multifaceted nature of intelligence. Emotional intelligence is just one of these other intelligences that are now considered important in understanding ability and potential.

Many cognitive skills taught in schools and used to measure IQ – problem-solving, for example – are separate from skills that deal with emotions. The stereotype of the genius who shows incredible intellectual abilities but is unable to relate socially is rare but does exist. The key to success seems to be finding a balance between rational intelligence (IQ) and emotional intelligence (EI); research by Professor Goleman and others has shown that those who are the most successful in life have high emotional intelligence and IQ. But whereas IQ can be pinned down with pen and paper exercises or online quizzes, EI is much more difficult to 'test'. What tends to happen is that psychologists test for a single component of emotional intelligence: so, for example, they can look at someone's 'empathy' skills by asking them to watch a video of facial expressions and describe what they think the person on film is feeling.

It's all in the mix

Although it is rare for someone of high IQ to have low EI, improving EI can often boost intellectual success. Because intellectual and emotional problems are more easily solved when we feel good about ourselves, and because self-motivated students tend to do better in exams, those with high EI often show evidence of intellectual success. They are also more likely to stay in education longer because they have strong networks of friends and can cope with the stresses of events such as exams.

On the downside, low emotional intelligence can limit intellectual performance. Just as many of us find we can't think straight when we're upset, so long-term distress can damage intellectual abilities and the capacity to learn. Depression, for example, can interfere with memory and concentration, while pupils who feel rejected are more likely to become aggressive and so are more likely to miss out on schooling. Research presented in 2002 by Roy Baumeister of the

Case Western Reserve University in Ohio found that feelings of rejection cut IQ scores by 25 per cent and analytical reasoning abilities by 30 per cent.

I'm convinced – so what about my school?

There seems to be no hard and fast rule about the best way of integrating EI into schools, but most projects start by improving the quality of all relationships: from manager to teacher, teacher to pupil and pupil to pupil. The best projects start with individuals committed to developing their own emotional literacy and gradually move on to working with colleagues and classes. Practitioners emphasize the importance of making the whole school community feel valued and supported, and giving everyone the chance to explore, understand and talk about their feelings. This may be with peer mediation and support schemes such as buddy systems (where older pupils act as listeners, friends and helpers to their peers), staff or pupil circle time (creating an open environment for discussion), a vibrant school council, or through visual and performing arts. More usually, it is through a holistic combination of projects and techniques, looking at everything from lunch hours to parents' evenings.

The important thing is to avoid scaring people with an over-zealous introduction of 'therapy-style' sharing sessions. And because teachers are not therapists or counsellors, it is also important that the work in emotional literacy is supported by specialist, intensive work with troubled children. But don't expect to turn your classroom into a haven of mutual respect overnight – most experts say that shifting the focus to emotional awareness is a slow process, and that it can take up to five years to have a discernible impact.

Chapter 14

Thinking skills

Plato and the Greeks knew all about it. The French know all about it now as it's been part of their curriculum for years. Thinking. That thing we do all the time. But do we do it properly? Learning to teach thinking skills has been made part of initial teacher training, and some schools have changed their whole programme of teaching to create opportunities for using thinking tools. Yet there's still no consensus about what thinking skills are, how they should be taught, or even if they're worth teaching in the first place. Are thinking skills just another initiative? Or are they the basis for an educational revolution that will change the way we teach and learn?

What are thinking skills?

Any use of the brain is a form of thinking, but when people talk about thinking skills they are usually referring to higher-order thinking. Higher-order thinking is when we use the brain for more than storing and retrieving factual knowledge. So, learning to reel off the kings and queens of England wouldn't involve higher-order skills, but devising a mnemonic to help you remember them would.

Broadly speaking, thinking skills fall into two categories – those rooted in philosophy, such as reasoning and logic, and those rooted in psychology, such as creative thinking and problem-solving. But behind all thinking skills is a strong emphasis on understanding the process of learning – on knowing how rather than what. The national curriculum lists five higher-order skills pupils should develop: information processing, reasoning, enquiry, evaluation and creative thinking. But some experts recognize as many as 30 separate skills.

At what age can children learn thinking skills?

Any age, according to those who approach thinking skills from a philosophical standpoint. But cognitive psychologists focus on two particular stages of development when the brain undergoes growth spurts: between the ages of 6 and 8, and again between 12 and 14. They argue that these are the key times for cognitive intervention to take place. They also believe that some thinking skills – such as abstract thought – cannot be acquired until the second stage of development, and that after the brain reaches maturity at around 16, acquiring new thinking processes can be difficult.

Opinion is also divided over the best way of fitting thinking skills into the timetable. Some people believe thinking is best treated as a subject in its own right, but the current weight of opinion is in favour of 'infusion'. This entails the teaching of thinking skills across the curriculum, by every member of staff, as part of a whole-school approach.

Can teaching thinking skills improve results?

It seems likely. The main body of evidence is centred on Case (cognitive acceleration through science education), a programme of teaching science through a thinking skills approach developed by a team at King's College London. The latest evidence shows that schools teaching the Case programme at key stage 3 go on to achieve 19 per cent more A–C grades in GCSE science than similar control schools that use traditional methods. Significantly, the Case students also achieve 16 per cent more A–Cs in English, and 15 per cent more in maths, suggesting that pupils have successfully transferred their thinking skills to other subjects.

Brain-based learning

It's not just thinking skills that teachers are being encouraged to explore. Many experts want us to look not just at how we think, but at how the brain works, and create a style of teaching that takes that into account. For example, experts often claim that the left side of the brain controls logical and analytical processes, while the right controls creative and artistic processes. Brain-friendly teaching tries to stimulate both sides, while recognizing that individuals have dominant areas and learn in many ways.

Another principle of brain-based learning is that tension or fear causes the part of our brain associated with learning to switch off. This leaves the part that controls primitive instincts, such as 'flight or fight', to take over. So children won't learn effectively if they aren't relaxed and at ease.

Other parts of the brain switch on only when they recognize they are about to learn something of direct personal importance. So brain-friendly lessons need a clear relevance to the pupils and a link to everyday situations.

Some terminology

So if you aren't there to give your pupils the answers, what are you there for? To encourage metacognition, create cognitive conflict and facilitate bridging, of course.

Metacognition, which occurs when someone becomes aware of their own thought processes, is considered central to almost any thinking skills programme. You can encourage this learning about learning by always trying to make the mental processes involved in the classroom explicit, and by encouraging pupils to keep a learning log to reflect on what they've been doing.

Cognitive conflict occurs when the mind is faced with new possibilities that perhaps go beyond its current lines of reasoning. As a teacher, you have many possible ways of creating cognitive conflict – by introducing new material to a class at key times, for example, or by playing devil's advocate during debate, or by constantly asking pupils to define terms, give reasons or expand on their initial answers.

Bridging is the name given to the mental process of taking thinking skills learned in one context and applying them in another. By linking your schemes of work in such a way that children can make connections, you can help them learn to bridge.

Although it's only in the past few years that thinking skills have appeared as part of initial teacher training, Robert Fisher of Brunel University, and author of *Teaching Children to Think*, is convinced that many teachers have been promoting thinking skills without realizing it. 'They have always developed thinking skills in their pupils – it's the natural instinct of a teacher,' he says. 'The difference is that they are becoming more aware of what they're doing.'

Giving the brain a workout

Teaching teachers to teach thinking is a huge industry, with dozens of companies offering their own programmes, workshops and training packages. Some offer subject specific schemes of work, whilst others focus on techniques – or 'thinking tools' – that can be applied across the curriculum. Some of these schemes and ideas are backed by research and evidence, but plenty aren't.

One of the best-known thinking tools is mind-mapping (also called thought-mapping or model-mapping), registered as a trade mark in the 1970s by Tony Buzan. It is a means of setting down information in a brain-friendly manner. A thought-map begins with a central idea in the middle of a page radiating out to major subheadings, then minor subheadings or individual facts. Thought-maps can be a useful tool for note-taking or revision, for thinking through a complex problem or for presenting information to others.

Another well-known thinking tool is Edward de Bono's 'six hats' which teaches children to view problems from a range of perspectives, and so develop a more rounded way of thinking.

Other packages use stories, puzzles or games to develop thinking skills. Word games or number games; two-minute teasers at the start of the lesson or more complex problems that may take a lesson to solve; lateral thinking or logical thinking; verbal games or physical games; tests of memory or tests of strategy. The list is endless.

Where to start?

The best advice is probably to ask around to find which workshops or materials other schools have found useful. If you do buy in training, keep an open mind – and don't treat everything you're told as gospel. There's probably someone else out there giving very different advice.

Chapter 15

Personalized learning

Personalized learning isn't a new concept. The 1944 Education Act obliged schools to provide 'an education appropriate to the abilities, aptitudes and needs' of every pupil. Back then, that meant segregating the high achievers from the strugglers. Today, it's different. In the twenty-first century, catering for the needs of individual pupils means tailoring lessons to different learning styles, giving pupils more choice and flexibility, and delivering learner-centred lessons that allow people to progress at their own pace.

What is personalized learning?

Personalized learning has been one of the defining concepts of education during the current decade. But what does it mean? To many, it conjures up images of children working alone at a computer or left to their own devices. But this is rarely the case. Instead, schools that champion personalized learning tend to share a common principle of trying to do the best for every child. 'Personalized schooling is about seeing each student as an individual human being,' says Derek Wise, head of Cramlington community high school in Northumberland. 'It's about adapting the system to the needs of the individual, rather than forcing the individual to fit the system.'

Learning styles

The idea that different children learn in different ways seems simple enough. But there is actually a great deal of confusion about how to define these different ways of learning. A recent research programme at Newcastle University identified 71 different tests on the market, all offering their own way of testing children and then classifying them into different learning groups.

One of the earliest classification methods was the Honey and Mumford system, pioneered in 1992. It identifies four categories of learner: activists, reflectors, theorists and pragmatists. Activists learn best when confronted with new ideas; reflectors prefer to observe others and listen to several viewpoints; theorists learn by drawing on their existing knowledge to analyse complex situations, while pragmatists progress by making clear links between the work in the classroom and life outside it.

More recently the DfES has promoted a classification system which divides children into visual, auditory or kinaesthetic learners – those who like to look, those who like to listen and those who learn best through physical activity, sometimes called 'active learners'. VAK has become the most widely used classification in schools, but there are plenty of other learning labels in use. Children can be deemed, amongst other things, to be adaptors or innovators, verbalizers or imagers, deep or surface learners, globalists or analysts.

The pros and cons

Learning styles enthusiasts argue that these distinctions help children to develop a greater understanding of themselves as learners. They also suggest that once teachers have identified the learning styles of the children in their class, they are better placed to deliver material in an appropriate way. The logic is simple enough – if material is presented in a format which matches the child's preferred learning style, then the child is more likely to be engaged and will find learning easier.

But some critics are concerned that many of the schemes in use in schools are unproven – often classifying children on the basis of quick questionnaires rather than in-depth testing. Others suggest that labelling pupils is unhelpful and that it may actually lead children to develop a limited view of their own abilities and to see themselves as only capable of learning in one particular way. They suggest that it may be more beneficial to think in terms of different types of *learning*, rather than different types of *learner*.

Should I change the way I teach?

Even if we accept that children learn in different ways, it's not clear how teachers should respond to this. Should you try to deliver learning in a way which matches a child's preferred style? Or should you deliver it in a different manner to try to stimulate the less developed ways of learning? In others words, is the aim to make short-term learning as easy possible, or is it, over time, to develop complete learners with a range of skills which can be adapted to all situations?

Most children perform better with some teachers than others and whilst this often comes down to subject matter or personality clashes, it may sometimes be the result of a teaching style not suiting a child's way of learning. Perhaps, rather than trying to work out the learning styles of your pupils, it might be more useful to analyse your own preferred way of learning – and teaching. Derek Wise encourages his staff to do just that, and to ensure that each lesson caters for the needs of visual, auditory and active learners. 'The obvious danger,' he says, 'is that your own learning style also becomes your teaching style.'

The personal touch

Most schools which claim to personalize education put a great deal of emphasis on giving each child individual attention, in and out of the classroom. For example, pupils at Lordswood girls' school in Birmingham, a comprehensive that topped the government's value-added tables in 2003, are attached to a 'review tutor'. The timetable is structured to allow these tutors to pull children out of lessons for regular one-to-one interviews. 'There are no form periods,' says headteacher Jane Hattatt. 'The focus is on the individual.'

In many schools, smaller learning groups such as study clubs, twilight classes, holiday courses and mentoring programmes are used to create opportunities for personalized learning. This is particularly useful when large class sizes make it difficult to spend much time working with individuals during regular lessons. Indeed, critics of the push for personalized learning sometimes see it as a response to the growing number of parents who already 'personalize' their children's education by using private tutors after school – or as an attempt to dissuade parents from opting for the independent sector, where increased personal attention is perceived as one of the main selling points. The staff-to-pupil ratio in independent schools is typically around 1:10 as opposed to 1:17 in the maintained sector.

Using technology

It's no coincidence that the rise of personalized learning has coincided with a surge in the use of information and communication technology (ICT) in schools. Technology can help personalize learning by guiding students through new material as and when they are ready to move on.

It may not be possible for one teacher to teach 30 separate lessons at several levels simultaneously, but it is possible for 30 personal computers to do just that. Critics argue that this kind of approach isn't all that different to an old-fashioned workbook, while enthusiasts point to a future of virtual field trips, online learning communities and lessons delivered remotely by world-class experts – with pupils able to design their own lessons to suit their individual needs.

Another feature of personalized learning is the use of ICT to track progress and identify individual needs. Technology now makes it easier to analyse data, monitor pupils' performance, and set individual targets. 'Personal target-setting has been one of the keys to our success,' says Jane Hattatt of Lordswood school. 'The targets are based on actual data, not on the opinions of the teachers, so it's entirely objective.' And it is not just test scores and exam results that can be entered into the system. Software company Connetix, for example, offers schools a package that allows them to enter a full day-by-day record of attendance, behaviour and achievement on a database that parents and pupils can access over the internet. Working alongside this is an online learning journal in which teachers, parents and pupils share comments and ideas. This kind of system encourages pupils and parents to become more involved in the learning process and allows staff to centre their teaching around the individual pupil.

Towards a school-free future?

Even if teachers are aware of learning preferences, the constraints of syllabus, curriculum and assessment, even of compulsory attendance, can make it impossible to offer a truly personalized form of learning. 'The whole school system conspires against personalized learning,' says Bernard Trafford, head of Wolverhampton Grammar School. 'All we can do is chip away at the edges.'

Some go further. Professor Roland Meighan, one of the United Kingdom's leading authorities on alternative systems of education, believes that genuinely personalized learning exists best outside schools, in the form of home education. 'The government's idea of personalized learning is a sham,' he argues. 'The programme of study is designed by the teacher, it is rarely led by the individual. A school's default position is always teacher-directed learning.' And some visions of the future hark back to the past. Former teacher John Adcock, author of *Teaching Tomorrow*, would like to see schools replaced by 'community learning centres' and teachers retrained as personal tutors who would oversee a group of around 20 children working independently for most of the time. 'It's not new,' he says. 'It's a return to the fundamentals of education that the Greeks drew up – a tutor and a group of pupils. The tutor would function in the same way as a medical GP, bringing in specialists as and when required.'

Whilst such a radical overhaul of the school system is unlikely in the near future, it does seem probable that there will be an ever-increasing emphasis on flexibility and independence. In the United States, for example, many states offer the option of flexi-schooling, where students spend some time in schools and some time working independently. Meanwhile, in the United Kingdom vocational choices are expanding, and some schools are even exploring the possibility of scrapping same-age classes and allowing pupils to progress as and when they are ready. In an age of consumer choice and customized products, the 'personalizing' of education is only beginning.

Chapter 16
Teaching children to read

Everyone agrees that learning to read is a good thing. But there's less agreement about the best way of achieving it. Because most of us don't remember learning to read, it can be easy to imagine there's nothing to it. But it's one of the most hotly debated topics in education – with its own bewildering jargon. Phonics? Whole language? Onset and rime? For parents and teachers helping with those first simple texts, it can seem a long way from the squiggles on the page to Harry Potter.

Baby talk

Learning to speak is the first step towards learning to read. There is still debate over how much language skill is innate, but it would seem that whilst reading itself is not a natural process, the ability to learn language is with us from birth. Babies have the ability to distinguish subtle sound differences and – unlike adults – they pick up a whole range of phonemes, the distinctive sounds used to form words. Each of the world's 6,000 languages uses a different assortment of these phonemes and, until six months, a baby's babble includes many more sounds than are used in their home language. After that, they begin to concentrate on the phonemes they hear most. Until the age of 1, babies hear speech as a series of distinct but meaningless words, but then they begin linking words to meaning. By 18 months they are boosting their vocabulary at the rate of one word every two hours. By the age of 3, they are beginning to 'play' with language by experimenting with rhymes. Learning to read is like breaking a code. Once children make the connection between the sounds they hear, the letters they see on the page, and the meanings attached to words, they've cracked it.

Sounds easy-peasy...

In theory, yes. But television and changing lifestyles mean parents talk less to their children than they did in the past. More children now arrive at school with poorly developed speaking and listening skills. In many European countries – particularly in Scandinavia – emphasis in the early years is on oral interaction; children may not be taught to read until the age of 7. But in the United Kingdom, the pressures of early-age testing and parental expectation mean schools start teaching children to read as soon as they arrive in reception class. The debate about the appropriate age to begin reading is a fierce one – and closely linked to an even fiercer argument over the best way to teach it.

At a basic level there are two models for teaching reading. One is sound-based, the other visual – or 'phonics' and 'whole language' as they are commonly called. But it isn't that simple. There are many approaches to phonics and whole language, and every approach has passionate proponents and entrenched adversaries.

Phonics: as easy as A, B, C?

The English language consists of 44 phonetic sounds, or phonemes. Phonics is a system of breaking down words into smaller components of sound. But there are several ways of doing this. The most commonly drawn distinction is between 'analytic' and 'synthetic' phonics. Synthetic phonics involves breaking words down (segmenting) into the smallest unit of sound, then teaching children to blend these sounds together to form words. So the word 'street' is broken down into five components: 's-t-r-ee-t'. This is sometimes referred to as 'all-through-the-word' teaching. Children are taught letters, and digraphs (such as 'th' or 'ee') and trigraphs (e.g. 'igh'). The idea is that children see the letters, make the sounds, and then blend them together to make the word.

Analytic phonics also involves breaking down words, but not necessarily into the smallest units. The onset-rime method, for example, divides words into openings and endings. So 'street' is broken down into 'str-eet'. Words are learned in groups or lists. The early emphasis is on initial sounds – so children might learn 'p' and then practise 'p-ig...p-at...p-ot'. Later, they tackle lists such as 'm-at', 'c-at', 'r-at', where the first part changes but the second is constant.

The academic evidence

Not surprisingly, there is a mass of academic research into reading – much of it unreliable. A review by the National Reading Panel (a US organization established by Congress in 1997 to monitor the effectiveness of a range of approaches to teaching literacy) of all research between 1970 and 2000 examined 1,100 reports. It found only 38 of these could be deemed 'valid scientific studies'. But interesting and well-documented case studies do exist.

Research carried out in Clackmannanshire, Scotland by Rhona Johnston (University of Hull), and Joyce Watson (St Andrew's University) has charted the progress of pupils following a synthetic phonics programme which was first run in the district's primary schools in 1997. At the end of the original 16-week programme, the children in the synthetic phonics group were reading and spelling seven months above their age, and seven months ahead of a control group who were taught analytic phonics. The progress of the children has been followed since, and has shown that the children who were taught synthetic phonics have stayed ahead, and that boys have matched the reading performance of girls, contrary to usual expectations. Results released in 2005 showed that at primary-leaving age the children raised on synthetic phonics had a reading age three years beyond what would be expected.

In the light of the Clackmannanshire research, the Government ordered a review of teaching methods. The Rose report (2006) came down on the side of synthetic phonics, suggesting the method be adopted by all UK schools.

Phonics: as slippery as fish?

While a phonics approach is the obvious way to tackle a 'transparent' language such as Swedish or Spanish, English is a minefield of irregular sound/spelling combinations. A Victorian advocate of spelling reform tried to demonstrate the absurdity of English spelling by suggesting that 'fish' could be spelled 'ghoti' – that's 'gh' as in 'tough', 'o' as in 'women' and 'ti' as in 'nation'.

At some point phonics will not suffice, and irregular words have to be committed to memory. (The counter-argument is that children taught phonics develop a closer eye for detail so are more adept at learning irregularities.) Another accusation levelled against phonics is that children learn to pronounce words correctly without knowing what they mean. (Phonics enthusiasts argue that learning to say the word is the first step, and that learning meaning follows after.) Critics also suggest phonics relies on 'direct instruction'; that it turns a creative process into a teacher-directed activity. (Equally, there are those who insist phonics can be fun if well taught.) Then there's the argument that unless children see a practical purpose to their learning they are unlikely to be motivated, which means using 'real' material, not tailored books which repeat a particular sound. (Critics of this view would point out that unless children learn to read efficiently, access to 'real' material will be limited throughout their lives.)

A visual approach: whole word and whole language

Many children start to read by learning their name. Because they learn the whole word, without breaking it down into sounds, it's known as the 'whole word' approach, and it works by familiarizing children with the shape of the word. The 'whole language' method shifts the emphasis away from individual sounds, even individual words. Instead, children are immersed in language and literacy through the sharing of books, games and rhymes. Later, they will be given books to interpret themselves, by relying on memory, intuition and the phonic knowledge they have picked up along the way. The books may be simple, but they will usually be 'real' in that they won't be tailored to a recently learned letter or sound. The emphasis is on uncovering meaning and this may well involve guesswork, sometimes prompted by pictures or by context.

Phonics purists don't like the idea of children being taught to 'guess', though there's an element of prediction and guesswork even in skilled, fluent reading. Reading sense, after all, is easier than reading nonsense – you, no doubt, just 'guessed' that 'Reading' at the start of this sentence meant the activity and not the town in Berkshire. Whole-language enthusiasts claim that this way of teaching encourages a stimulating classroom environment where children learn creatively. But it can be daunting for those who struggle to read, or who don't get opportunities to practise at home. There is also the danger that children rely purely on memory – only to find as they get older that they lack the skills of working new words out for themselves. The counter-argument is that a child who learns through a whole-language approach will still be phonemically aware because children instinctively pick up phonemic rules and apply them.

So why not mix and match?

In reality, this is what a lot of teachers do. Most experts agree that phonics teaching has a role to play, but many believe there is more to literacy than phonics alone. A systematic teaching of phonic knowledge can easily be combined with a holistic approach that immerses children in language.

The argument for using a variety of methods is simple: different children learn in different ways. Widely held, though not conclusively proved, beliefs include phonics suiting boys best, girls favouring whole-language methods; left-brain dominated children preferring phonics, right-brain liking 'real' books; high-achievers flourishing under a whole language approach, low-achievers benefiting more from phonics instruction. The important thing, if taking elements from both phonics and whole language, is to ensure that your approach is still structured and systematic, rather than a muddled mixture of ideas.

Where does the National Literacy Strategy fit into all this?

The National Literacy Strategy (NLS) was launched in 1998. Its cornerstone, literacy hour, decreed that primary schools would provide structured literacy teaching for one hour every day. But what type of programme does the NLS offer? The answer is a bit of everything. There is a phonics element, although experts are divided as to whether this is of the analytic or synthetic variety. The consensus appears to be that there has been a shift towards synthetic, a shift which is likely to continue in view of the recent Rose report, which advocated synthetic phonics being taught 'first, fast and only'. Opinions vary as to how successful the NLS has been. Literacy rates across all age ranges have improved over the past five years, but on the other hand girls still outperform boys and there are still large numbers of children who are not learning to read proficiently.

Reading the past

The literacy debate is not new. The phonics movement has roots in the mid-nineteenth century. By 1898 a phonics programme, devised in the United Kingdom by Nellie Dale, was popular on both sides of the Atlantic. But with the introduction of large comprehensive classes, the authorities decreed that 'look and say' methods were the easiest way forward. In the 1920s the most popular resource was one-word flashcards, but these were soon replaced by reading schemes and by the 1960s, 'Janet and John' type books were in almost every school.

It wasn't until the early 1990s that phonics began to regain popularity in the United Kingdom with the appearance of several resources, such as Jolly Phonics by Sue Lloyd, which set out to make phonics more enjoyable and accessible. Since 1998 most schools, though by no means all, have followed the NLS with its eclectic methods. The most popular current reading resource, used in about 75 per cent of primaries, is the *Oxford Reading Tree*, a series of illustrated stories that originally leaned towards a 'look and say' approach. But pressure groups such as the Reading Reform Foundation – which advocates systematic nationwide teaching of synthetic phonics – have kept the learning-to-read debate high on the education agenda. And rightly so. Not only do poor readers have difficulty gaining academic qualifications, they also face the social stigma of illiteracy, as well as missing out on the joys of reading for pleasure. And whilst experts say that 75 per cent of people will learn to read regardless of how they are taught, that still means one in four will struggle.

Chapter 17
Promoting creativity

The Tokyo-based think tank, the Nomura Institute, believes the development of human society has evolved through four 'ages'. We have passed through the age of agriculture, the age of industry, and that of information, and are now said to be entering the age of creativity. But what is creativity? If you think it's something to do with starving artists in draughty garrets, think again. Creativity is about finding original solutions to everyday problems, helping young people to express themselves and equipping the next generation to find work in a rapidly changing world.

Big C or small c?

Creativity is a slippery concept. The ancient Greeks believed creative inspiration was a gift from the gods, and even today some educationists see creativity as the preserve of the chosen few. For example, Howard Gardner, the Harvard professor who founded the concept of multiple intelligences, defines creative people as 'those who make a difference in their chosen domain'. But this elitist notion – 'the Big C' theory – is less popular than it used to be. Most experts now offer a more democratic definition.

Creativity is not the hallmark of greatness but a human characteristic which we all share, albeit to differing extents. 'Being creative means having original thoughts,' says Dennis Sherwood of the Silver Bullet Machine, a consultancy for business innovation based in Rutland. 'And with the right stimulation almost anyone can have an original thought.' The DfES has a similar, if less romantic, view. It stresses that the creative process must be 'purposeful', 'directed towards achieving an objective', with an outcome that is 'of value in relation to that objective'. In other words, creative ideas don't just have to be original, they also have to be useful. Since it's so tricky to say exactly what creativity is, it's worth saying what it is not. Creativity is not the same thing as academic ability, and indeed many creative children often fare badly in exams. Nor is it the same thing as talent, which refers to aptitude and skill, but not necessarily to originality.

Can you teach creativity?

Yes. At least, you can encourage it, nurture it and develop it; although, as with anything, some children will take to it better than others.

A 2003 Ofsted survey of 42 schools found that one in five was 'exceptionally good' at promoting creativity. Jane Loder, head of Ashmead school in Aylesbury, Buckinghamshire, one of the schools singled out for praise, says that creativity is best developed in every aspect of school life. 'It's a generic approach, a way of working that encourages open thinking, different outcomes and new ways of expressing yourself. We're strong in art, dance and music – but that's only part of what we believe creativity is about.'

But there are those who believe that rather than trying to promote creativity, schools should simply focus on not destroying it. Experts have found that children have high levels of innate creativity, and are naturally imaginative. But research in the United States by K.S. Meador in the early nineties found that the sharpest drop in children's levels of creativity was between the ages of 5 and 6 – or when they first went to school.

Will there be a job at the end of it?

Creativity, it seems, is a highly marketable commodity. The 'creative industries' are the fastest growing part of the British economy. They employ around 1.4 million people and contribute more than £100 billion each year to the UK economy. But it's not just about TV, advertising and film; even traditional businesses are putting an increased emphasis on 'thinking outside the box'. In a recent survey by the Work Foundation, corporate bosses identified 'recruiting and managing creative employees' as one of the five key factors for business success. And that's unlikely to change. The rapid progress of technology means it's estimated that 60 per cent of the jobs that today's primary children will do have not yet been invented, so the capacity to be flexible and free-thinking will be increasingly important to their job prospects. It might also be important to their future happiness, since creativity has been shown to help people cope better with problems in their personal life, as well as in the workplace.

Call in the feng shui expert...

For whatever reason, our ability to be creative seems to be linked to our surroundings. Just as artists or writers may find a landscape or studio that proves to be their inspiration, so children seem to draw creativity from their physical environment.

What makes a good creative classroom will vary from subject to subject. Do the display materials reflect the value placed on creativity? Do the seating arrangements encourage children to interact with each other? Is there easy access to working resources? Make sure that the room doesn't feel cluttered. And remember that a change of environment can often stimulate creativity; do lessons always have to take place in the same classroom, or even in a classroom at all? Alsop high school in Merseyside has developed a series of 'creative learning spaces' including a history room with stage and costumes so pupils can re-enact key historical moments.

And it's not just the working environment that is important. Play has an important role in developing creativity, so recreational space also needs to be looked at. Millfield primary school in Norfolk has developed a creative outdoor classroom with sound sculptures, circular spaces and sit-and-chat areas. 'The space determines how children behave and learn,' says headteacher Cathy Parkinson. 'Before this we had eight acres of open field, yet oddly it was a restrictive environment.'

Beyond the curriculum

The main stumbling block to promoting creativity is the need to cover the national curriculum. There is far less emphasis on creative development within our national guidelines than in other European countries, whilst in the Far East 'creative thinking' is often seen as the bedrock on which the whole of learning is based.

But while our national curriculum may be restrictive, it is not an insurmountable obstacle. An increasing number of schools are experimenting with a timetable based on projects rather than subjects. At St John's school and community college in Wiltshire, for example, learning in Years 7 and 8 takes place through modules. A typical topic might be 'What makes us unique?', with subject specialists called in as required to teach information directly relevant to that topic.

'It's coherent, continuous, and it makes work a creative exercise,' says headteacher Dr Patrick Hazelwood. He says that children who have been taught this way performed 'significantly better' in national testing in maths and English than a control group, despite the fact that the school's first step in designing the modules was 'to throw out the national curriculum'.

Even if you're not brave enough to plunge the detonator on your working practices, it may be possible to experiment. Oakham school, an independent secondary in Rutland, for example, has designated project weeks each term, when children work in groups to tackle creative challenges such as composing a school anthem, recording a radio programme or building a totem pole.

But a knowledge-based curriculum isn't necessarily the enemy of creativity. New ideas don't come out of nowhere; they are usually born out of a sound working knowledge of a subject, and an understanding of the ideas of other people. Traditional learning and creativity certainly aren't mutually exclusive.

Tune in, tune out

Brain bank connectivity (BBC) is the term used to explain the creative power of a group of people being greater than the sum of its parts. The theory goes that if there are two people in a discussion, then there are actually three opportunities for a creative idea to arise: from person A, from person B or from the creative link between them. With more people involved, the number of links expands exponentially, increasing the likelihood of original and exciting ideas. Enthusiasts argue that getting children to work in groups encourages 'blue-sky thinking' by helping them to overcome the barriers that normally limit their way of looking at problems.

But teamwork is only one outlet for creative inspiration. The idea of the creative thinker needing a bit of peace and quiet also has its supporters, among them children's writer Philip Pullman, who has called for recognition by schools of the 'more private, solitary nature of creativity'. Finding time for children to be alone in a busy school isn't easy, but there may be possible solutions; working outside in summer or creating private study areas. Try canvassing children's own ideas about what helps them shut out distractions and become absorbed in their thoughts – even if that means listening to music on their iPods.

Sit down, shut up and be creative!

Sometimes the biggest obstacle to creativity in the classroom is the person at the front of it. Teaching creatively and teaching in a way that encourages creativity are two different things. It's possible to design an ingenious lesson on Tudor history, only to deliver it in an instructional way.

The expectations teachers have in terms of pupil behaviour can also act as an obstacle to promoting creative thought. Research shows, for example, that children labelled 'creative' have a higher than average chance of getting into trouble with their teachers.

Arguing with the teacher, shouting out impulsively, and refusing to let an issue drop are all possible signs that a child's creative urge has been awakened. But when creativity has a proper focus it should lead to an orderly working environment, rather than an unruly one. Indeed, schools that are committed to promoting creativity, usually report that children show a huge improvement in terms of attitude, self-esteem and social skills.

In practice

The discussion in the headteacher's office is about effective learning. Phrases such as 'success criteria' and 'thinking skills' trip easily off the tongue. But this isn't a posse of visiting DfES officials, nor even the senior management of a forward-thinking comprehensive. It's a group of 9 and 10-year-olds at Huntington primary school in Staffordshire.

'When I arrived here five years ago we tried to work out what we wanted the school to be,' says headteacher Clare Robertson. 'We wanted to give the children ownership of their learning and allow them to be creative. But we didn't know how we were going to get there or what it would look like in the classroom.' And what does it look like? 'It looks like fun. And it sounds like excitement, with lots of noise, talk and laughter.'

The timetable at Huntington is itself the result of creative thinking. The teaching year is divided into five seven-week blocks, each structured around one of the five thinking skills outlined in the national curriculum: evaluation, creativity, information processing, enquiry and reasoning. During each seven-week period, all the work delivered in every subject focuses on one of these skills.

From scientific inquiry to historical investigation, the 300 or so children at Huntington learn explicitly that skills are transferable. Except for literacy, numeracy, RE, music and PE, which remain on the weekly timetable, subjects are taught in blocks, with as many trips and outings as possible. So children may have three weeks of science all afternoon followed by a fortnight's geography.

'It means a deeper kind of learning can take place,' says Ms Robertson. So what's a deeper kind of learning? 'We had several bags of dead mackerel here last week,' she explains, part of a two-week art project involving close observation and ICT research into underwater life. It has produced imaginative drawings, paintings and models. The Year 3 fish artists are enthusiastic about developing ideas over an extended period. As one of them says: 'Sometimes imagination takes a long time to happen.'

Creative, co-ordinated timetabling of this kind relies on staff working together. The single post of deputy has been replaced with four team leaders, each in charge of a separate age group and all these leaders and their teams are freed from teaching for half a day each week to develop joint ideas while their classes are taken by teaching assistants.

'We're not afraid to give anything a go,' says Lesley Bennett, team leader for Years 1 and 2. And so brain gym, meditation tapes, philosophy classes and t'ai chi all feature, while classrooms have a 'peace bowl' filled with smooth stones and a candle. What do parents in this traditional former mining village make of it all? 'One or two asked us what the point is,' says Ms Bennett. 'But when they see the work the children produce, they're happy. If we are educating the whole person and developing creativity, we can't ignore the spiritual side.'

Huntington pupils talk frankly about their work, which they are encouraged to mark themselves and children also have a 'learning interview' with Ms Robertson, where they reflect on how they learn best, which teaching styles they respond to, and what difficulties they have faced. Asked to identify possible obstacles to learning, one child suggests a particular class is too noisy. Another complains that one of her teachers shouts.

'As soon as I started interviewing the children about their learning I thought, 'Why have I never done this before?' says Ms Robertson. 'They have all the answers.'

Part III

The well-rounded classroom

All the issues tackled so far can contribute to making a fruitful and stimulating learning environment. But why stop there? For just a little bit of extra effort – and with the right support – it's possible to turn a good classroom into a fantastic one. This section explores some of the ways to boost the quality of classroom life. A visiting poet, a resident dog, a solar panel or two – all of these can help make the school experience more satisfying for you and more memorable for your pupils.

Starting a school council, creating an overseas link or redesigning your school, however, is usually more than any one teacher can manage alone. It requires co-operative working, management backing and, often, a slice of the budget. But while this kind of whole-school approach is important, more often than not it's the drive of one teacher which gets the ball rolling. A bit of passionate enthusiasm and hard work may be needed to get a project started. With the right support, it will soon take on a life of its own.

All the issues in this section are examples of ideas which have flourished in recent years. Partly, this is as teachers have grown more aware of the learning potential in long-term, cross-curricular projects. Partly, it is the recognition that incorporating activities like recycling or pupil elections in everyday classroom life helps teach children responsibility to themselves, other people and the planet.

Chapter 18
Going green

Need a bit of extra cash for text books? Then try switching off the lights or flushing with rain water. Government figures show that some schools face energy bills up to 60 per cent higher than others, while some pay twice as much for their water than their cost-conscious peers. But it's not just about saving costs. With global warming, the disappearance of fossil fuels and increasingly stretched landfill facilities, schools are being encouraged to do their bit for future generations.

On the right track

The green school campaign starts well outside the school gates – 40 per cent of primary and 20 per cent of secondary pupils are driven to school, most travelling less than two miles, even though a national survey published by the Department of Transport in 2002 found that 80 per cent of children would like to walk to school given the chance, and 65 per cent of parents would prefer not to have to tackle the stressful taxi-run every day. A year later, research by University College London, showed that children got more benefit from walking to school every day, than from a weekly two-hour PE session.

The good news is, that with grants available for schools with a complete travel plan, and childhood obesity being so much in the news, more and more schools are encouraging children to walk or cycle, either alone or as part of a walking or cycling 'bus'. Research published by the sustainable transport charity Sustrans in 2005 showed that schools which have had time to properly implement their travel plan show a 20–25 per cent reduction in car use.

Getting people out of the comfort of their cars is never easy but there are some simple steps schools can take. With each child making an average of 4,000 journeys to and from school over the course of their education, even small changes can make an incremental difference. Having good, secure cycle storage and safe access points for pedestrians is a start, and taking time to explore the whole issue with parents should forestall some of the angry letters from committed car users. Sustrans recommends appointing a 'school champion' who can take responsibility for a complete review of transport in and around school, and each local authority has a school travel adviser who should be able to offer advice on issues like parking restrictions, footpath widening and lighting, speed limits, traffic calming or extra crossings.

Money down the drain?

Schools spend around £70 million a year on water, an average of over £2,500 per school. A large secondary can spend as much as £20,000 – and typically flush water accounts for 40 per cent of consumption. But a few simple measures can save water, and money. Check for leaks and get the flow reduced on your taps, swap to taps which shut off automatically after use or change to spray heads, which use 50 per cent less water.

And even if your crumbling 1960s building doesn't allow for hi-tech rainwater flushes in the toilets, swapping old-fashioned urinal flushing systems which sluice water day and night (and through the weekend) with intelligent flushing systems, can make a real difference. Finally, keep an eye on your meter. If you read it last thing at night and first thing in the morning, it will show up whether leaking pipes or dripping taps are wasting water overnight – and large meters attract bigger standing charges than smaller ones, so once you've reduced consumption, installing a smaller metre might save even more money.

Eco-Schools, an environmental project founded after the Rio Earth Summit in 1992 and which works with over 4,500 registered eco-schools in the United Kingdom, estimates that a package of small water-saving measures can save a school of 600 pupils around £5,000 a year. More importantly, involving the pupils in monitoring water and using the information for classroom projects promotes green habits.

Or just money to burn?

There are more than 40,000 school buildings across the United Kingdom, consuming a quarter of the public sector's energy costs. As with water, there are some big savings to be made: some school heating systems waste 40 per cent of the energy they burn. And estimates from Encams suggest that £100 million a year of public money could be saved if schools were to become more energy efficient. Schools in the sunny south might like to consider solar energy: Ilfracombe community college in Devon installed eight solar panels in 2004. A bit bleaker up north? Then why not consider wind power – the United Kingdom is Europe's windiest country. Cassop junior school in Durham became the first wind-powered school in Britain when it installed an 18 metre, 50 kilowatt wind turbine in 1999. On windy days the system even exports extra energy into the national grid. It may be worth noting, however, that such technology should be regarded as a long-term investment: it will take Cassop 25 years to make a profit on installing their turbine.

Looking after the pennies

But there are savings to be made and even small changes can free up money in a cash-strapped budget: changing regular light bulbs in your classroom for special energy-saving bulbs, for example, can save £10 per bulb per year. Turning down the heating thermostat by 1° can reduce bills by 10 per cent. Closing doors; turning off lights in unused rooms; re-arranging after-school clubs so that they're not scattered around school and turning computers off rather than leaving them on screensavers can all save energy. As part of its Action at School programme, Global Action Plan has been working on small practical changes with 20 schools and has seen an average saving of £9,400 per year, with some bigger schools saving £15,000. It points out that, because most classrooms are poorly run in terms of energy use, even simple measures can make a real difference.

If the thought of some extra cash is not incentive enough, then naming and shaming the wastrels may spur them into action – new European legislation should soon mean that all schools will have to publish their energy consumption figures. Using this as a model, some schools have taken the same tough stance and published league tables of classrooms, awarding 'blacklist' points for offences such as lights left burning or wasted heating.

Waste not, want not

Although about half of our waste could be recycled, we currently manage only around 12 per cent. And with landfill sites quickly becoming full to overflowing – and studies showing associated health risks from living nearby – that means more environmental damage from incinerators or rubbish dumps out at sea. Research by Eco-Schools found UK schools spend £39 million a year on collecting litter, £56 million on emptying bins and £150 million on stationery. Which means a lot of potential for recycling – even when the figures are not quite so substantial. Minsterworth primary school in Gloucestershire has just 52 pupils, but growing mounds of waste still left them with the choice of either buying a bigger bin each week or getting sorted on the recycling. Choosing the recycling option not only saved them around £20 a month, but got the children into a good habit. The impetus for Minsterworth's recycling project came when they entered a competition to design a recycling system for drinks cans. Now classrooms have baskets for recycling paper, packaging, ink cartridges and mobile phones, as well as aluminium foil (which can fetch around £300 per tonne) which goes to help fund a local adult learning centre. Other schools have also successfully installed facilities for composting fruit waste, or sold on plastics to recycling companies. As with everything, environmental groups emphasize a 'small is beautiful' approach to recycling – reusing envelopes; using both sides of sheets of paper and making double-sided photocopies; reusing folders; working with electronic documents, and making sure those empty water bottles don't go to waste.

Tricky teenagers

Although many primary schools are geared up for tackling green issues in the curriculum, organizations often find it more difficult to run successful projects with secondary schools. This can be because of fewer cross-curriculum opportunities and because pupils tend to feel less ownership of particular rooms or buildings. But it's also an age thing. Teenagers can be disappointing when it comes to responding personally to green issues: the biggest litter-dropping offenders, for example, are teenage boys. Research by Encams which runs the Keep Britain Tidy Campaign as well as Eco-Schools, found that because young people are the biggest consumers of crisps, fizzy drinks, sweets and the like, they are also the biggest litter bugs. In particular, they found that teenagers tend to be instinctive litter bugs. On the whole they seem to feel no guilt about discarding their rubbish on the streets, and don't see litter as a big issue.

Getting cleaned up

If litter is a problem around school – and in most schools it is – the first step is to embark on a thorough survey to find out where most rubbish is being dropped, when and by whom. Then you can begin to tackle the hotspots. Some schools have found that shrubberies and hedges not only catch all the litter blowing around in the wind, but are more likely to attract rubbish from pupils who regard them as surrogate bins. Re-designating the tired shrubbery as a wildlife garden and spending money on better plants and landscaping may help change perceptions while giving your school an immediate resource for 'green' education.

It may seem obvious, but the next step is to take a good look (and smell) at your bins. Are there enough? Are they emptied regularly? Are they in the places where pupils and staff tend to eat and socialize? Are they easy and pleasant to use or are the lids stiff, narrow and grubby? Are they big enough? Getting bins with the right capacity might mean the difference between emptying twice daily or twice weekly. Be imaginative with your bins. Be willing to move them around to see where they are most effective. Once you've got pupils, and staff, into the habit of using bins, it's easier to persuade them to differentiate between different sorts of waste in a recycling campaign.

Getting results

For some lucky schools, the green tomorrow is here today. Kingsmead primary in Northwich, Cheshire, for example, which opened in September 2004, is constructed mainly of timber, rather than metal and concrete. It has an emphasis on natural light, uses recycled woodchips for fuel, collects rainwater to flush the toilets and is heated by solar energy. The 'intelligent' green building can close windows if it rains, open them when a classroom becomes too stuffy and draw blinds if the sun seems too strong. In the grounds, pupils grow organic vegetables for the kitchen staff.

Research shows that 'designing-in' these kind of green features may have knock-on effects in the classroom. Work by Professor Cedric Cullingford at Huddersfield University and Brian Edwards, Professor of Architecture at Edinburgh College of Art, has found clear links between the design of buildings and pupil attainment – in the 'green' schools studied for the research, SATS results improved by 2 to 4 per cent, Ofsted reports were generally more favourable than for comparable 'non-green' neighbours, and absence rates fell. The results were particularly striking with primary children who tended to stay in the same space all day. The study – largely based on schools in Hampshire built between 1984 and 1996 – showed that 'green' schools cost around 12 per cent more to build but suggested they were worth the extra expense. In schools built with natural materials teachers displayed less stress, pupils were more relaxed and parents felt more welcomed. The research also found that some of the most common elements of 'green' building design had accidental benefits besides their environmental justification. Central atriums, for example, designed to control light and air flow became important social areas, encouraging a sense of community, providing space for displays and allowing informal teaching.

Environmental or sustainable?

One of the big advantages of tackling green issues, is the material it gives for curriculum work. At Kingsmead primary the whole building can be used as a giant teaching resource. Water pipes are transparent so that pupils can track the flow of rain water, and classroom laptops are linked to the main computers which control school conditions so pupils can get to grips with how it all works. Even the CCTV has a life beyond security patrols, acting as cameras for watching wildlife in the grounds. But even without the advantages of a new-build school, environmental organizations have plenty of advice for using practical changes for curriculum ideas, from developing sculpture trails in outdoor spaces, to recording energy consumption data and researching renewable resources.

The only difficulty might be in deciding what to call your new curriculum packages. There's some debate about where 'environmental education' ends and 'education for sustainable development' begins. Or whether, in fact, they are the same thing. Basically, environmental educationists tend to focus on practical green issues, and encourage field trips and hands-on activities, while education for sustainable development (ESD) is often seen as having wider implications about social and economic development both in the United Kingdom and abroad. Most green projects involve a bit of both, but ESD is now a compulsory component in the curriculum for science, geography, design and technology and citizenship, and the DfES has funded the Qualifications and Curriculum Authority (QCA) to develop a website which includes curriculum material for incorporating ESD into a range of other subjects.

Small steps on a big planet

Many environmental organizations are convinced that schools are beginning to green up. They recommend regularly measuring figures for waste and energy consumption so that improvements can be tracked annually and it becomes clear what steps are making a real difference.

This helps boost morale – and shows up where schools might need to ask for help.

Even if your school seems stuck with the energy-guzzling ways of the past, it doesn't mean you can't make a difference. According to environmental organizations, it's usually one teacher's enthusiasm which kick-starts a green project. This often begins in a small way in the classroom and gradually spreads the word to other staff and pupils. The key to long-term success seems to be getting everyone at school to buy into the idea by getting green projects fixed into the management plan, and sweet-talking the bursar!

In practice

When I became citizenship co-ordinator in September 2003, the school was in decline as regards litter. We had received complaints about pupils dropping litter in the streets and in the nearby shopping complex, and Darlington council was about to name and shame the school. At the same time, a group of students complained to me about the state of the school grounds. It was time to tackle the problem.

The first thing we did was bring together the school council reps, who arranged for a survey of the school to identify litter hotspots. These turned out to be near the tuck shop, dining room and in two copses of trees where pupils congregated. We invested £1,000 in new bins, which were strategically placed where the survey had highlighted a need. The school council also went to the shops to ask owners what they saw as the root of the problem, which turned out to be not only pupils dropping litter, but a lack of waste bins in the shopping complex and on the route from school. Bins that were in place were not emptied often enough, resulting in overspill of litter and food waste.

We asked the council, through the community services department, to partner our fight against litter. They helped us with posters, which we put up round school and at the shops. They provided extra litter bins between the school and the shopping complex, and they agreed to empty the bins more frequently. They also provided materials for litter-picking safely: rubber gloves, overgloves, pick-up sticks and fluorescent jackets. Now our lower-school forms take it in turns to do a week's litter picking. The environment has been transformed. When we changed our school day we had to move litter picking from afternoon registration time to morning registration. We employed an extra caretaker, part of whose duty is to help keep on top of the litter that accumulates after lunch.

We've been lucky in our partnership with the council, but the key has been to change the pupils' attitude towards litter and the environment. Litter picking used to be a punishment. Now we emphasize the positive side of it, and they see it as helping the environment and the local community. We also stressed the health and safety hazards of having litter around school. I did a series of themed assemblies about the problem and the possibilities of litter causing disease and encouraging rats.

We're proud to have been awarded a Darlington council environment award for our success in tackling litter. We have also won a Healthy Schools award for increasing pupil participation; we recently appointed two pupil governors to put forward pupil views on improving the school, and are setting up a schools council website, specifically to address pupil issues. Whether or not we are successful in these innovations will not stop the ongoing process of making the local environment an important issue with pupils. We hope this will raise awareness of global environmental issues as well as concern for the local community.

Roger Sharpe is head of history and citizenship co-ordinator at Hummersknott school and language college, Darlington.

Chapter 19

Using volunteers

According to the National Centre for Volunteering, nearly a quarter of all voluntary work in the United Kingdom is carried out in support of schools. That's six million volunteers each giving an average of four hours every week. Or a billion hours of help each year. All in return for nothing more than job satisfaction – and the occasional free school lunch. Much of this support is behind the scenes as parents help to raise money or organize the summer fete. But volunteers are increasingly taking centre stage – on the governing body, in the playground and, not least, in the classroom.

The legal obligations

The DfES states that criminal record checks are not compulsory for volunteers working in schools, unless they have unsupervised access to children. However, a growing number of local education authorities are requesting full checks from the Criminal Records Bureau. And from 2007, schools may be able to make instant on-line checks on volunteers. Whatever the practice in your area, disclosures will reassure parents and make volunteers feel they are being treated in the same way as staff. And it won't cost you anything – the CRB doesn't charge for checks on volunteers. But it's your own vetting procedure that matters most. If you're appointing a volunteer who isn't known to the school, insist on references, just as you would for a paid employee. And even if volunteers have been cleared by the CRB, as a general rule they should not be left unsupervised with children – particularly in a one-to-one situation.

Make sure volunteers are aware of basic health and safety regulations, and check that your insurance covers them, particularly for sports activities or when transporting pupils. Finally, it's good practice to offer to pay expenses, but make sure it's done out of petty cash. If you offer volunteers a regular weekly sum, however small, it can be interpreted as a wage. Not only will this interest the taxman, it can also be legally construed as a contract of employment.

The moral obligations

Volunteers work for nothing, but they aren't free labour. It's a fine line, of course, but the message from the unions is that volunteers should not be used to plug shortages, only to supplement existing staff. The NASUWT stresses that volunteers should not 'undermine the professional standing of trained staff, whether teaching or non-teaching'. In particular, teaching assistants and ancillary staff can feel threatened if volunteers are asked to work alongside them doing a similar job for no money. 'If it's mums coming in and cleaning up paint pots, then fine,' says a spokesperson for the public service union Unison, 'because that's not what TAs do. If volunteers are helping with literacy, for example, it can be more awkward. But so long as they are used in addition to paid assistants and not instead of them, there's no problem.'

Difficulties can usually be avoided by having a clear policy on volunteering, outlining how and why volunteers are going to be used, and explaining the benefits. Volunteer Development offers a helpful code of conduct on the issue of 'job substitution', the golden rule being that 'volunteers should not be doing work that was formerly carried out by a paid employee or is still carried out by a paid employee'. Having some kind of evaluation plan will allow you to assess whether volunteers are making an impact – and will reassure staff that you're looking to raise standards, not cut costs.

Pushy parents

Parents – especially members of the parent teacher association (PTA) – are often the first to put up their hands for other voluntary work. It's important to harness that enthusiasm and not to offend your champion fundraisers. But be warned: parents don't always make the best volunteers. The charity Volunteer Reading Help has a policy of never placing parents in their own children's school, and while some heads believe that having mums and dads around adds to the sense of community, others feel it creates unease. 'There was an instance of one parent reporting back to the PTA about what she saw as the weaknesses of the teachers she'd been working with,' explains one head. 'Staff felt they were under surveillance.'

One way around potential problems is to team up with a nearby school in a 'parent–volunteer exchange'. Although parents are keen to help 'their' school, most will see the benefits of a partnership. Alternatively, make use of parents around the school, but not in the classroom. Certainly, having parents working with their own children's class is best avoided.

Tracking down volunteers

Parents aside, volunteers usually fall into three categories: students, those working in local businesses and retired people. Several organizations run schemes putting volunteers into schools: some specialize in particular skills, such as reading support, while others provide general help. Using one of these groups means recruitment is done for you, and most of the organizations are experienced at matching volunteers to schools. Some training is also usually provided as part of the scheme. The only downside is that most of the charities report that demand outstrips supply, so they may have no recruits in your area. But it's worth a try.

Schools that handle recruitment themselves often find a strategically placed flyer or poster can be more effective than advertising in the local press. Libraries, adult education centres and student unions are all potential recruitment areas. It's also possible to get help from your local volunteer bureau – a kind of job centre for those seeking voluntary work.

Write to local businesses, but be wary of companies that nominate employees for duty. Unsuitable 'volunteers' often turn out to have been press-ganged by bosses who think it boosts the corporate image. By asking businesses to do no more than display a leaflet on their notice board, you will make sure only those who are genuinely interested will apply. As a general rule, target the immediate vicinity. Those who live or work close by are most likely to volunteer, and most likely to prove reliable.

Word of mouth is your most important recruiting sergeant. If volunteers have a positive experience of the school, they will encourage friends to get involved.

What can volunteers do?

That depends on the individual. The trick is to find a role that suits the school and the volunteer. All schools have one organized and committed body of volunteers – the governors. Most have a second – the parent teacher association. As far as in-school volunteering goes, the two most common contributions are general classroom assistance and one-to-one reading support. Some volunteers – such as artists, writers or sports people – bring specialized skills. Others adopt mentoring roles, providing personal and pastoral support. But not all volunteers want direct contact with pupils; many are content simply to pick up litter and stack chairs, answer telephones or work in the library.

And what can't they do?

Volunteers are not qualified teachers, and they're not being paid. Everyone needs to be realistic in their expectations. Volunteers should never be left alone with a class, for example, or pressured into doing more than they want to. One volunteer recalls being asked to mark homework – not surprisingly, the person refused. But equally, volunteers like to be kept busy. They are giving up their time, so they don't want to feel it's being wasted.

Volunteers at the top: the governors

There are 370,000 school governors in the United Kingdom – the largest organized volunteer workforce in the country. They devote an average of 180 hours of their time each year, and for the chair of governors a year in office can be virtually a full-time job. It's not just the meetings, it's work carried out on the school's behalf, time spent on training courses, and involvement in school events. It's little wonder that recruitment and retention of governors can be difficult: around 10 per cent of governor positions are vacant, and in London the figure is double that. It can be particularly difficult to attract 'co-opted' governors who have no personal link with the school, even though a growing number of large employers are encouraging staff to become governors by offering them extra days of paid leave. Having empty chairs at the board table is more than just a burden for those left making decisions; it can also cause practical problems. Latest regulations demand that a governors' meeting must have an attendance of 50 per cent, plus one, to be quorate. This can make it difficult to get through business.

Even though they are volunteers, governors shoulder a considerable load: they are responsible for policy-making; they have a duty to write behaviour guidelines, set up home–school agreements, implement complaints procedures and set targets for performance. They also play an important role in considering exclusion cases and administering performance management pay for teachers. The governing body is the agency through which the school is accountable to the local education authority for use of public money, the character of the curriculum and the organization of staff.

Perhaps not surprisingly, in annual surveys carried out since 1999 by the National Association of Governors and Managers (NAGM), governors have said their responsibilities and workload are too onerous for part-time volunteers and many professionals suggest payment may become necessary, if only some kind of allowance for the chair.

The most effective governing bodies tend to be those that reflect the background of the pupils in the schools, although this is not always straightforward: in London, for example, 47 per cent of pupils are from ethnic minorities, but only 23 per cent of governors. Training is available through LEAs, and, as part of the National Strategy for Governor Support and Training launched in 1999, the DfES provides specialist training for new governors, although research suggests that only around 60 per cent of new governors take up the offer.

And while you might think governors have little to do with day-to-day classroom life, this need not be the case: governors need interaction with pupils as well as staff if they are to understand the school. In some schools, individual governors are linked to particular classes or departments, which they visit regularly, getting to know the teachers and understand pupil learning. Others invite governors on 'pupil tracking' exercises, where they follow one child throughout the school day. And governors can always try to persuade pupils to sit on their committees. Those who have done so report that it's not only a good learning opportunity for the child, but by far the best way for the governors to get to know the pupils and hear their concerns.

Not just for primaries?

The majority of volunteers work in primary schools. Primary school parents usually have more contact with their schools, and volunteering often seems like a natural progression from doing the school run and marking up gym kit. At secondary level, it's a different story. Larger schools mean less personal contact. More parents are in paid employment, and sensitive teenagers can be horrified at the prospect of having a parent around school. The National Association of Parent Teacher Associations, however, says an increasing number of secondaries are encouraging parents to get involved, with developing a strong PTA often the first step. They point out that sometimes it's down to heads to make the initial move and make it clear to parents that they would be welcome.

But there's a definite fear factor, especially among non-parent volunteers who may be swayed by popular media images of poor school discipline and threatening behaviour. Luring them across the threshold can be tricky. But if you can manage to get them into school to see things for themselves – perhaps with a special social evening or a personal invitation to a school event – then they may well prove the most loyal of volunteers. Research by Community Service Volunteers has shown that those who take the plunge and choose secondary schools have some of the most positive volunteering experiences.

Getting the most out of volunteers

A 1997 survey by the National Centre for Volunteering found that more people are prompted to volunteer because of their 'own needs' than because of the 'needs of the community'. With that in mind, the first step is to find out what volunteers themselves want from their involvement.

The next step is to define what you expect from them. Don't just assume that as long as you have volunteers in school, then you must be doing a good thing – it's best to be clear about what each volunteer is going to contribute. Schools with many volunteers – and some have 20 or more on their books – usually appoint a volunteer co-ordinator. This may be a member of staff or a volunteer, and the individual's role is to ensure there's a clear focus to what each volunteer is doing and that they don't get in the way of staff.

It's a good idea to have a handbook. Volunteers will need basic facts about the school – parking, toilets, lunch arrangements, fire drills and so on – as well as information specific to their role. Explain clearly the standards the school expects in terms of confidentiality and conduct. And always try to treat volunteers in the same way you would treat any other colleague. It's important to make them feel they are a part of school life, even if they appear for just half an hour on a Wednesday afternoon. Inviting them to special assemblies and school events can help them feel included. The lack of material reward means volunteers appreciate gratitude even more than regular employees.

They're not teachers

The most common concern of new volunteers is what they should do if confronted by difficult behaviour. They need to know, for example, if they have any disciplinary powers. One of the great strengths of volunteers is that they are not authority figures, and it's best to keep it that way. Ask them simply to report bad behaviour to a teacher, rather than get personally involved. Similarly, it may be appropriate for volunteers to use their first names rather than a title.

It's because volunteers aren't teachers that they can bring something new to school. But the lack of barriers can also cause problems. It can become easy for children to become emotionally attached to a volunteer, especially if they're doing one-to-one work, and volunteer induction or training should flag up the risks of a child becoming too dependent on them.

Is there any training for volunteers?

Volunteers make such diverse contributions to school life that it would be impossible to offer general training to suit everyone and it usually comes down to special arrangements between individuals, schools and LEAs. But organizations that run volunteer schemes often provide some level of training, even if it's only a few hours. And some offer far more extensive opportunities. Bexley Education Business Partnership, for example, runs a 10-day course called Helping in Schools, accredited by the National Open College Network and involving practical and written assessment. Perhaps best served are the schemes for reading support: almost all of these offer volunteers at least two days' training in teaching literacy. Unfortunately, as most of the training for volunteers is carried out locally, the only way to find out what's available is to ask around. As well as individual charities, try your LEA and local volunteer bureau.

Just how valuable are volunteers?

If the hours of voluntary help in schools were charged at the average national wage, the volunteering contribution would amount to £10 billion a year. Yet the real worth of volunteers is difficult to gauge, not least because they fill such a variety of roles.

Research in 2000 by the University of Sunderland, for example, found that using volunteers to provide reading support had no impact on standards. 'Having more adults in a classroom meant things got fragmented,' says Professor Julian Elliott, who headed the research team. 'Many of the volunteers lacked expertise, and there was surprisingly little liaison between staff and volunteers.' Not everyone accepts this view, however. Volunteer Reading Help cites its own research, which found that after a year of support, 23 per cent of the children improved their reading age by two years, while 89 per cent increased their self-confidence.

Regardless of whether or not volunteers help to raise standards, there is no doubt they make a positive contribution in other ways. They can provide children with positive adult role models, promote an ethos of citizenship and emphasize the value of education. Volunteers also enjoy their work. A survey as part of the United Nations' International Year of the Volunteer in 2001 found that volunteering was the second most pleasurable activity in people's lives – after dancing. So having volunteers in schools has got to make them happier places.

Chapter 20

Artists in residence

It took Michelangelo four years to paint the Sistine Chapel. Film director Peter Jackson worked on his *Lord of the Rings* trilogy for seven years. And Philip Larkin only published a major collection of poetry about every decade. Creativity, it seems, can't always be rushed. Which is why more and more teachers are taking time to work on long-term projects with artists in residence. Squeezing a few extra bodies into the classroom or tinkering with the timetable can be a small price to pay for getting in step with contemporary dance or shuffling your stanzas with a professional poet.

What is a residency?

Having an artist, or a group of artists, in school to do a half-day session is a workshop; working with them on more sustained projects over weeks, terms or even years is a residency. Depending on who you choose, and how you agree to work, a residency can be anything from developing an on-site sculpture to making a film or creating an opera performance.

Does size matter?

While an afternoon's workshop may seem a lot less hassle, the longer the project, the more the possibilities. Smash and grab workshops can be refreshing, but without building up a rapport between the artist and school, they can also feel like a token gesture. This is particularly true of art forms which might take a bit of getting used to. A half day of contemporary dance, for example, is hardly enough to stop the giggles, let alone break into a sweat. Short workshops can be fraught with the newness of the art form and it's sometimes not until you get beyond the initial barriers that work really begins to develop.

But I teach science!

Art and drama classes need not get all the fun. Many schools have developed ways of using artists across the curriculum. A good residency is not just about learning specific skills, like life-drawing or arpeggios, but about introducing lateral thinking and cultural exchange – which can take place in any subject. A variety of recent projects have highlighted the benefits of bringing art into other disciplines: the 'strangebedfellows' project, for example, at the radiology and physics unit of the Institute of Child Health at University College, London linked sculptor Marion Kalmus with neurophysiologist Mark Lythgoe to produce a hybrid that was part artwork and part scientific research.

At Birchfields primary school in Manchester, a new curriculum was introduced in September 2004 with artists in residence at its core. Making everything from Indian music to films, the children now have the opportunity to take part in cross-curriculum projects throughout the year. 'You just have to think differently,' advises Julie Howell, performing arts co-ordinator. 'You have to get used to the idea that you can use history time in conjunction with arts time, and that's OK as long as there's an outcome for both.'

Good for them

Residencies seem to be good all round. They encourage creativity in the classroom, offer new ways of looking at the curriculum and can be particularly good at unlocking the potential of pupils who find more traditional teaching styles a turn off. Collaborations between artists with different skills – perhaps bringing together a painter with a dancer, for example – can be especially effective. It can help children to see the connections between art forms and opens different doors for different children. It reinforces the message that there's more than one way to express an idea and can spark a whole range of questions. Sometimes there may even be knock-on effects. Never thought of a career as an opera singer? Then perhaps you didn't have the right role model. Organizations who regularly work on residencies, like English National Opera, suggest that getting children intrigued in a new skill can be the first step in helping them realize that it's possible to make a career in the arts.

It's not only the children who benefit, however. A good residency also gives the artist the opportunity to focus on their own work. As well as the creative activity of working with classes, time away from the studio or practice room can offer a valuable research opportunity which gives artists the chance to develop and explore their own practice.

And good for you

Teachers who work in residencies are overwhelmingly enthusiastic about the professional development opportunity it also offers them. While getting an artist into your classroom can seem like an added burden in an already hectic life – and can be a daunting prospect for the first-timer – it can be extremely rewarding. At Yateley school in Hampshire, a specialist arts college since 2002, they have already welcomed theatre and dance companies in residence as well as individual dancers and actors. 'It does take a lot of time to make it work,' suggests Nickie Harrison, head of drama. 'But once you've got it organized the benefits completely outweigh all that. It's not just that these performers have advanced skills that we don't have. It's also good for us to sit back and see how our classes respond. It gives you an opportunity to look at what you do objectively – and find new ways of doing it too.'

Counting the costs

But all this creativity comes at a cost. This can vary from several hundred pounds for working on a short-term project with an individual artist to thousands of pounds for more ambitious projects: buying in the full company of the Scottish Dance Theatre for just one week's residency, for example, could set you back £9,000. It's best to be realistic about fees – residencies are not a way of getting cheap labour, and the better funded your project is, the more likely everyone is to get worthwhile results. A useful guideline is the Arts Council's 'approved rate' for artists which suggests the kind of day-rate you should be considering, but if there's something you fancy but think you can't afford, try talking it through with the artists themselves. There are usually options, like sharing a residency with other schools, linking with local arts festivals or changing the format of what's on offer. Experienced artists will have worked through many of these alternatives before and can offer advice.

Reaping the rewards

There may be ways of raising money to help. Local arts organizations and your regional office of the Arts Council should be able to give advice on what kind of funding might be available – it could be anything from a DfES scheme to a grant from a local charitable trust. One of the main tasks of Creative Partnerships, administered by the Arts Council but set up jointly in 2003 by the Department for Culture, Media and Sport and the DfES, is to help find a way through the bewildering maze of funding opportunities.

Unfortunately, all this takes time. Which means not only planning well in advance, but also considering the workload. At Birchfields primary, Julie Howell was freed from classroom teaching for two years to develop their programme and admits that without that time it would have been 'very difficult'. If this is just not possible, then it's still worth making sure colleagues know just how much is involved in organizing a residency so that they don't also sign you up for all kinds of other jobs.

Another option might be to draft in some extra help with the form-filling. The PTA at Belper Long Row school in Derbyshire took responsibility for raising funds for a year-long sculpture residency in 2004, applying to its local Arts Council office for support. They found the application process simpler than they had expected, enjoyed the buzz of working with artists, and have now undertaken to organize a residency for the school every three years.

Getting started

The key to a good residency is finding the right person for your project, someone with whom you feel comfortable and who fits the ethos of the school. But how do you get the match-making right? The best way is to draft in help from an expert arts organization as early as possible, to help match an artist's expertise with the expectations of the school and make sure it turns out to be a genuine collaboration rather than a one-sided crusade on your part.

Having found your artist, you might like to give some thought to the brief. Too vague and you risk misunderstandings and disappointment. Too tight and the artist may feel they are being restricted. It's a question of getting a balance between what the artist wants to do and the outcomes the school would like to see. This usually means talking to the artist in advance of making the final brief so that they can have some input. If they are not genuinely interested in investigating the ideas behind the residency then you might end up with little more than a bit of classroom decoration. Try experimenting with an open-ended brief which might allow the final 'product' to emerge during the residency itself rather than stipulating in advance that you require a sixteen-foot high, green and orange striped elephant for the nature garden. This means trusting the artist to thoroughly explore ideas with the pupils – and there may be an element of risk – but it might make for a more creative process.

From signing up to cleaning up

Planning a residency is not easy – and it's worth being aware of some of the pitfalls so that you make sure you can avoid them. The Arts Council publishes a guide to best practice called 'Artists Working in Partnership in Schools', which goes through everything step by step. This includes, among other things, making sure everyone is signed up to a clear contract; checking your insurance cover; making sure the artist has had their police checks and asking them for a risk assessment; getting the residency into the timetable; arranging classroom support; drumming up parent enthusiasm and warning the cleaners and buildings supervisor about the probable mess.

It takes two to tango

Though it might seem tempting to find a quiet corner in the staff room to work it all out, it's wise to involve the artist as much as possible, and as early as possible, in the whole process. They'll probably have helpful hints from previous projects and it should raise any issues which need ironing out. 'At the beginning of a residency I set up a hands-on workshop with all the staff after school. It's a bit of fun. There's usually lots of wine and cakes. But it means everyone knows who I am, what I'm doing and what I'm expecting of the school,' explains Coralie Turpin, a textile artist and sculptor based in Sheffield. And what does she expect? 'A proper space to work. Often I'm stuck in part of a corridor, or, worse still, moved around from one place to another. It shows a lack of respect.'

Depending on the type of residency, volume of space may not be everything: some schools may have massive halls but with hard floors which are unsuitable for dance, for example. Getting these practical basics sorted in advance can save a lot of trouble later on. 'It's also important to have a single member of staff co-ordinating – and that they let other teachers know what's going on, where and when,' says Ms Turpin. 'Otherwise I end up running round looking for children, which is a waste of my time.' Anything else? 'Overalls. Oh, and it's really nice if someone makes you a cup of tea on your first morning. It makes you feel welcome.'

Where can I get help?

There are lots of organizations which can offer advice on hosting a residency. Unless you know the ropes, probably the best first port of call is your regional office of the Arts Council. There will be specialist staff for all the different art forms who have information about artists working in your area, examples of previous projects and details of funding opportunities. They can also put you in touch with your local Creative Partnerships schemes.

But there are other routes: Long Row PTA, for example, put an advertisement in *The Stage* magazine and were delighted with the response. Many cities have 'open studios' weekends where you can visit local artists and talk to them directly about your ideas. Or if you know of a theatre, dance or music company you want to work with, try approaching them through their education staff. But getting the support of a specialist arts organization may be just the thing to give your residency wings. They can help with materials, scheduling and fundraising, so that the final project is probably much bigger than the school could have managed on its own resources alone. Residencies can easily fall by the wayside because schools are overstretched and under-resourced. Drafting in someone with experience of managing big projects can be the difference between success and failure.

In practice

We've been running an artists in residence scheme for 14 years. The bursar allocates enough money to employ someone for eight months a year, and we can be flexible about how we use it. Usually we have two artists for four months each: long enough for the school and the artist to get used to each other, and for the artist to make an impact. Some of the very successful residencies we have extended beyond four months.

A rota system gives all the arts subjects a turn. We've had photographers, painters, songwriters, sculptors, puppet makers, lighting designers, theatre directors, set designers, writers, computer artists, composers and a maker of automata. We find people by word of mouth, by a chance meeting or by trawling the internet and making a few calls. When we find someone we like the sound of, we invite them to school to discuss the sort of work they might like to do. Then, if we still like the look of each other, we arrange a formal interview before making an appointment.

The main aim of a residency is to fire up enthusiasm among our students, but there's also an element of old-fashioned patronage. We want the artists to pursue their own projects, as well as working with us, and we hope the residency will give them the necessary time, space and financial security. For example, Greg Norminton completed his first novel during his time here, and has gone on to establish himself. In turn, the school benefited from the workshops he led, and from plays he wrote for our first-year pupils.

We pay our artists around £750 a month and we offer accommodation too, though sometimes people prefer to travel in. If it's appropriate, we also buy a piece of work from the artist to give a permanent reminder of the residency. We're privileged to be able to afford to run a scheme like this: it enriches the cultural life of the school. We try to offer good value to parents, and the residencies are money well spent.

Inevitably, some ventures are more successful than others. One or two haven't quite worked, not through any fault of the school or the artist, just because things haven't clicked. When they work well, they can be stunning. One memorable residency was with musician and raconteur Jeremy Taylor, who used a small choir and an organ to produce a musical piece based around Ted Hughes' poems. And it's always good to see a lasting impact. Pete Churchill taught huge numbers of pupils to sing gospel music with enthusiasm, and broadened the school's appreciation of jazz. Playwright Jane Buckler worked particularly with younger children, directing them in a couple of plays; as that year group grew up they retained a real passion for drama and became a mainstay of the school's theatre.

We have a talented staff at Wellington, but students sometimes think a teacher is just a teacher. If someone is making a living from their art, it's obvious they are good at what they do. So they get enormous respect. A subtext of any residency is inspiring students to think of a career in the arts and to see the artist as a role model. And they are also wonderful development opportunities for staff. It is always inspirational to watch a professional in action and explore new ways of doing things. When a residency works well, the artist is a cultural example to the whole school community.

Anthony Peter teaches English at Wellington College, Berkshire.

Chapter 21
The learning environment

Traditionally, schools were modelled on the factories of the industrial revolution. But while most other legacies of Victorian education have gradually been replaced, school design has altered little in over a hundred years. With the government promising that all secondary schools in England will be rebuilt or refurbished within the next 15 years, things are beginning to change. The Building Schools for the Future project has seen over £2 billion shared among 180 schools during the first phase of the programme in 2005 and 2006, with more to follow. It should bring schools and communities together with leading architects. It could even spell the end for draughty mobiles, smelly toilets and crowded corridors.

What is good design?

Some design elements are subjective. Are you a glass and steel enthusiast or a natural materials buff, for example? Do you like the cool and uncluttered or the homely and welcoming? But good design is about more than looking attractive – its' about working properly. Well-designed schools should be efficient, robust and flexible. The design process should take account of everything from how the school sits in its plot of land and how it is accessed, to the colour of the corridors and the way the lockers work.

While recent years have seen significant changes in our understanding of how children learn, school design has struggled to keep pace with these more sophisticated approaches and there has been little detailed research about what makes the best learning environment. Pilot initiatives by the DfES, such as Classrooms of the Future, have helped focus attention on what could be done and specialist organizations like the Design Council have helped schools experiment with everything from designing for different learning styles to introducing 360° classrooms with swivelling chairs and wall-to-wall whiteboards. But there is still a long way to go.

Out with the old

A standardized, institutionalized environment, lacking character. Add-on technology squeezed into classrooms. Uncomfortable, inflexible furniture. No control over light or ventilation. Regimented desks. Cluttered social spaces. Noisy and overcrowded. Sound familiar? But the traditional classroom environment is not just uninspiring. The Design Council's Kit for Purpose research in 2002 showed that poor design in schools reduced the range of possible teaching and learning styles, undermined the value placed on learning, wasted time and increased maintenance costs. And a Mori poll conducted in 2004 found that 95 per cent of teachers recognized that the classroom environment had a strong influence on the way children learn and behave.

Despite this, most staff also believe school design is unchangeable and beyond their control – something to work around rather than something which could be used more positively. To some extent this is the result of practical experience, but it is also the product of years of design conditioning: it is because our ideas of what a school should look and feel like are so culturally deep-set that they have changed so little over the past century or more.

And in with the new

The Building Schools for the Future (BSF) project, launched in 2004, with the aim of rebuilding or regenerating all secondary schools, has already set aside £2.2 billion to be shared by around 180 secondary schools in 14 local authorities. More funding is promised and the DfES hopes that at least three schools in each authority will have begun a major remodelling by 2016. As part of the scheme a special organization, called Partnerships for Schools, selects bids from LEAs and works with project teams on the management of the BSF process. Some of the projects are managed conventionally, while just over half are subject to partnership agreements with the private sector along the lines of existing private finance initiative (PFI) agreements. In Scotland too, school design is high up the political agenda: the Scottish Executive published guidance on design issues in 2003 and hopes to rebuild or refurbish 300 schools by 2009.

Light and airy?

So if your school becomes part of a redesigning process, what can you expect to end up with? The brief for many school design projects emphasizes flexibility. That way they can be easily updated to take account of changes to teaching styles, ICT requirements, pupil numbers or community use. Swapping a single monolithic building for a series of clusters, for example, each with classrooms and social spaces, is one way of getting this flexibility. This allows certain parts of the site to be accessed for adult learning or after-school activities without opening and heating the whole school; it can separate younger from older pupils to help them feel more secure and it can accommodate slot-in 'pods' for extra classroom, storage or office space. The recent emphasis on extended schools means we may be heading more towards mini-villages than the concrete warehouses of the past.

Inside, new designs often emphasize break-out spaces where children can interact in small groups and replace dingy corridors with light-filled atriums. There is enough space for staff and pupils to move around comfortably and the long treks from one side of school to the other – or even one site to the other – are reduced. Many new designs use sustainable materials, have an emphasis on natural light and ventilation and include sculptural elements, landscaped grounds and 'intelligent' lighting, heating and toilet systems which can respond automatically to changes in conditions.

Or cheap and noisy?

Inevitably, however, design conflicts and budget restrictions also have a role to play. Replacing cramped classrooms with large open-plan spaces, for example, can make it difficult for designs to comply with acoustic standards, which can have a knock-on effect on health, behaviour and attainment. Rapidly changing requirements like those for ICT can also cause problems. While plumbing and lighting go in as a school is being built, ICT often goes in at the end with the desks and curtains, which can mean power sockets in the wrong place and trailing leads. Worse still, the technology may be out-of-date before it's even been switched on.

And what's the point of a shiny new school if you get backache from the old chairs? Although children sit on school chairs for 15,000 hours of their lives, a survey in 1995 found 86 per cent of furniture in some schools was unsuitable for use. According to charity, BackCare, little has changed in the intervening decade and over half of children are experiencing back pain as a result of poor seating. While European manufacturers frequently develop furniture in partnership with schools, many UK manufacturers still do not comply with the existing British Standard for school furniture.

Making a difference

Getting your classroom refurbished, and thinking hard about layout and design, may have more benefits than just providing nice photos for the prospectus. At Bexley Business Academy in Kent results went up from 6 per cent of five As–Cs at GCSE to 36 per cent after their new building was opened in 2004, while at Kingsdale school in Southwark, remodelled with a budget of £11 million over six years from 1999, results rose from 15 to 41 per cent of five As–Cs between 1999 and 2002.

And it's not just the number-crunching which seems impressive. Better designed schools have been shown to improve behaviour, promote staff communication and encourage more use by parents and community. Better light and ventilation can cut sickness; good acoustic design helps improve concentration and save teachers' voices while use of robust, sustainable materials can reduce bills. If further proof were needed of getting a return for your investment, take a look at the stock market: the FTSE 100 companies that are most design-savvy outperformed the rest of the stock market by 200 per cent over ten years.

In the classroom

Before getting carried away, many organisations recommend a sober look around the classroom as a first starting point: take a detailed audit of what does and doesn't work and what extra basics you need, and then move on to looking at how different layouts, equipment or furniture could be used to boost your teaching. Changing the configuration of chairs and desks can alter the whole feel of a room, and whilst shifting furniture around between lessons isn't an appealing prospect, it's true that different layouts suit different classes or different kinds of lesson. Clusters of desks for group discussion, circles for class discussion, desks perhaps facing out to the walls for when pupils are doing individual work. Make sure the chairs are comfortable and weed out any that have seen better days – it's surprising how often fidgeting is the result of physical discomfort rather than boredom.

Then there's your own desk and chair. Is your desk a barrier between you and the class? A place you retreat behind when you're feeling tired or fed up with the lesson? Perhaps – in a spirit of solidarity – you should use the same type of desk and chair your pupils have, rather than a flashy teacher's version? Then there are practical considerations in the layout of the classroom. Does everyone have space to write comfortably? Is it easy for you to circulate around the room and check on progress? Studies show that teachers spend most of their time in the front of the room, at the centre, often because a cramped classroom makes it too tricky to move around. The most important thing is to experiment, rather than feel that you have to work around the existing layout of the classroom.

In the staffroom

Getting classrooms right, and having effective public spaces, is only part of the design conundrum, however. A study published in 2000 by Jane McGregor at the Open University showed that teachers had modest ambitions for their staff spaces – a clean kitchen area came top of the wish-list, followed by a quiet workspace with good computers, telephone links and a photocopier – and yet in many cases staff rooms were so unpleasant that teachers preferred to remain rooted at their desks.

And while it might not seem to matter if people choose to brew up in departmental offices or skulk in the smokers' room, a dysfunctional staff room may have a knock-on effect. A fragmented staff which only meets up for formal meetings is unlikely to collaborate well: an empty staff room isn't just a physical absence, it can demonstrate what goes on at a deeper level in the school. A well-designed staff room can get people talking and encourage a more relaxed and friendly environment.

Recognizing this, the Teacher Support Network tries to encourage teachers to step off the treadmill occasionally and make more use of staff room facilities. They point out that spending time and money on a decent staff room, helps counteract the idea that anyone sitting down for a five minute breather cannot be pulling their full weight. Getting together informally can also break what the Teacher Support Network calls 'the conspiracy of silence'. If there are no opportunities to socialize, then it's easy for individual teachers to think they are the only ones having any problems. A pleasant staff room environment can make it easier to take a step back and look at solutions with colleagues, rather than feeling inadequate.

Getting help

If you want to look at ways of improving the design of your classroom, staffroom, departmental corridor – or whole school – but don't know your atrium from your buttress, or your purlin from your pointing, where can you get help? Aware that teachers often don't have the time or expertise to research the best design solutions, many organizations offer advice and support. The Commission for Architecture and the Built Environment (CABE) can appoint an 'enabler' to help demystify the process and get schools and contractors talking the same language. The Design Council also offers expert advice, some inspirational models and practical help. In a similar vein, SchoolWorks publishes a 'toolkit' to help guide schools through the nuts and bolts of the design process, while the Scottish Executive and Children in Scotland have a number of practical guides.

Chapter 22
School links

With global citizenship firmly established in the curriculum, more and more schools are forming partnerships outside the United Kingdom – with ten times as many school links now as there were in 1999. Using e-mail, web-cams, satellite phone links and virtual tours, these are a far cry from old-fashioned pen pal exchanges. But how do you find the best link? And once you've got one established, how do you get the most from it?

What is a link?

Hopping across the Channel to brush up on French verbs may be important for language skills, but is not a school link. 'Linking' refers to a formal, long-term and equal partnership with another school, often, but not exclusively, in a developing country. It can include everything from regular e-mail contact between students to reciprocal visits and themed social events. The important thing is that the link is not a one-off extravaganza for the end of summer term but makes useful, frequent contributions across the curriculum.

Vegetarian, non-smoker, GSOH – how do I find a link school?

Finding a partner is easy, and there are plenty of matchmakers out there. Although some schools use local businesses or communities to provide links, most go through a specialist organization. These usually have bases in a particular country or area and an established network of schools. Some provide a free linking service, while others charge for ongoing support. The UK One World Linking Association (UKOWLA), for example, provides free advice and support to encourage links in Africa, Asia, Latin America and the Caribbean, while Link Community Development, runs a programme involving more than 400 schools in Ghana, Uganda and South Africa and more than 250 in the United Kingdom. It asks schools for a four-year commitment of £500 a year: for this it provides information packs, curriculum materials and long-term support, as well as initial help in finding a partner school.

The British Council is also committed to helping school links. It manages programmes which offer grants, develop best practice and provide advice and support, both through websites and regional workshops and training days. The British Council resources provide advice on finding a link as well as a special 'dating agency' section for schools seeking a partner. Although it's not important to 'match' your school exactly with another, it makes life easier if you share the same expectations, have compatible communications technology, and are working with students at the same key stages.

Getting connected

Most schools keep in touch with a regular programme of letters or e-mails. Some invest in satellite links or videoconferencing equipment. Don't underestimate communication difficulties – most African schools, for example, won't have e-mail; phone calls are expensive and mail may be unreliable or even have to depend on the diplomatic postal system. Getting an intermittent response (or even none) to friendly missives can be discouraging, so it's worth getting as many systems in place as possible before you start. And, of course, the most popular and effective way of consolidating a link is by regular and reciprocal teacher and pupil visits. All schools agree that there's nothing to beat face-to-face contact for making the link work.

The secret of success

Links are often the brainchild of an individual teacher, and when that member of staff moves on or gets too busy, the link can fail. It's better to get the whole school involved and generate widespread enthusiasm so that linking becomes part of the ethos of the school.

Quite often, partner schools start the link with different ideas about what it will involve. In the most successful and sustainable relationships, both take time at the beginning to discuss exactly what they want from the programme, how it will work on a practical basis, and what they are prepared to commit to the scheme. Perseverance is also important. Links need to be seen as a long-term commitment rather than a one-off activity to meet curriculum targets. Be warned that the initial stages can be frustrating and time-consuming, and it may be several years before the link starts to work as you would like it. Both schools need to build confidence and there can be a settling-in period while they try out different activities and get them built into already action-packed school programmes.

What will my school get from it?

While the link is a good basis for the global citizenship curriculum, it can be much more. The school link between Polesworth high school in Tamworth, Warwickshire, and Pampawie junior secondary school in Ghana, for example, has been running since 1999. Polesworth find linking is particularly important for schools such as theirs which are largely rural and have few opportunities to experience other cultures and communities. Since the link was set up, 11 staff from Tamworth have made the trip to Ghana and Polesworth has played host three times to visitors from Ghana. On a practical level, it's produced material for everything from geography projects to food technology research.

Linking can help bring to life different cultures, races and religions; introduce issues of justice, trade and economics; provide professional development opportunities; and simply remind pupils and staff that there's a wide world beyond the exam room. But the benefits may not be confined to school. Many participants find the link a good way of getting more involved with their local communities, choosing links with countries represented at their school. Others find it a good way to draw in local business support.

And what about the other school?

Linking is not just about raising money for schools in developing countries. In fact, many programmes steer away from any aid relationship. Oxfam would rather fund-raising were not part of linking at all: it points out that it is hard to avoid developing a condescending relationship if children are always raising money to help those they see as poorer. Instead, Oxfam encourages link activities like visits and exchanges which create active connections rather than emphasize differences.

Despite these reservations, many link schools do raise money for their partners, often providing computer equipment and teaching resources. But although the impact of these practical improvements is easy to measure, it's the less tangible outcomes which may well be most effective. British Council link officers in each country report that a good quality link with a UK school boosts the self-confidence of the link partner, that teachers are more likely to remain for longer – providing greater stability – and that students demonstrate higher academic standards.

Is funding available?

There is unusually good news here. First, linking need not be expensive. In the beginning, all that's needed is an exchange of letters, e-mails, photographs or school work to enable curriculum activity to be built around the link school.

On an even brighter note, a range of grants is available. These vary depending on where your link school is, and what kind of work is being done. A good starting point is the British Council, which has an overview of what's going on and which administers a variety of grants as well as offering funding for curriculum development once the link is up and running. As with all grant applications, it can be worth getting the paperwork done as soon as possible. Those who run school links recommend finding funding to send staff out to the link school at the outset of the project, so that the whole experience becomes real and personal rather than just another curriculum activity. The key is getting a core of staff fired up so they can pass on their enthusiasm to everybody else and keep the link moving through more mundane times.

What are visits like?

The first visits are usually made by staff, paving the way for student exchanges later on. A visit from the United Kingdom to the link school typically lasts about two weeks, with the travellers staying with local families and often shadowing family members to get real experience of everything from domestic chores to health clinic appointments. Visits are rarely about exchanging teaching skills so much as agreeing practical steps to make the link work.

Although some time might be spent observing or teaching lessons, most of the visit will be taken up in meetings. When staff from Polesworth first went to Pampawie, they met the community chief and elders, the district director of education, the diocesan bishop, the parent teacher association, staff from the British Council, the Ghana International Bank and other local secondary schools, the district assembly and international aid foundations. If the visit is by pupils, it might include group meals, outings or sports matches – and often the UK pupils work alongside their hosts at a practical project. Children on visits to Gambia and Ghana organized through UKOWLA have, for example, helped to build classroom blocks, decorate workshops and fence a mango orchard.

What support can we expect?

Because linking is such a growth activity, there's plenty of support available. Again, the British Council is a good first port of call: it heads a consortium of organizations which offer a variety of specialist advice. The Cambridge Education Foundation offers guidance to teachers on getting accreditation for all the hard work involved in making a successful link – research and practical projects could count towards anything from a postgraduate certificate to a masters degree – while VSO has put together a global educators' register. Making use of some of the thousands of returned volunteers who have worked in schools outside the United Kingdom, the register brings together anyone interested in working on linking and puts teachers in touch with those who can share useful information and resources.

The Department for International Development also encourages teachers to make contact with their local development education centre to access resources and support. The centres work under the Development Education Association and can provide training as well as informal support and information for link schools.

Specialist linking organizations, too, know the ropes and can be helpful in offering practical advice such as how to apply for grants or how to build the school link into the curriculum. Link Community Development, for example, offers staff the opportunity to share experiences and information, and runs an annual conference to highlight some of the issues around linking.

What happens if we fall out?

The drop-out rate for linked schools is low. And if partnerships do fail, they tend to fizzle out rather than explode in a series of angry letters.

But there can be difficulties. These are often the result of simple pressures – technical problems about communication, other commitments using up the time needed to make the link work, a change of staff or disappointment arising from unrealistic expectations. Like all relationships, there can be rocky patches, but if you have made the partnership through an organization, there will be plenty of help to see you through. Support staff in each of the link countries can visit the schools to iron out practical difficulties or help arrange more realistic activities. If the breakdown is irrevocable, then they will help to set up a new link.

Does the link have to be with a school in a developing country?

Not at all. Although many of the government initiatives (and hence the grants, too) are directed towards linking with schools in developing countries, many successful links have been set up elsewhere. Japan 21 organizes partnerships between the United Kingdom and Japan, with its own grants scheme and specialist support. Schools in the United States are also popular.

And old-fashioned though it might seem, there are still lots of good links to be made in Europe. Costs of visits within Europe are generally lower and funding is available through the European Union. For those wanting to test the water, a European link can be a good starting point: most European schools are already familiar with the mechanics of exchanges and it can be easier to develop a good curriculum project which is clearly understood by both partners.

Some schools like linking so much that they have partners in more than one continent. Kelvin Hall school in Hull is working with schools in St Petersburg, Sierra Leone, Transylvania, Germany and Estonia, and has won the British Council's International School Award. 'It's all about being more outward looking,' says Claudia Lorenz, the school's linking co-ordinator. 'It's about being aware of yourself as part of the wider world. It doesn't matter about the type of school or where it is. What matters is getting an international perspective into the classroom.'

In practice

Bemrose secondary school in Derby has 700 students who speak 46 different first languages between them, from Persian to Portuguese. At Highfields school in nearby Matlock, there are 1,500 students, but the only first language is English. 'The two schools are in the same county, with just 22 miles between them,' says 18-year-old Alex Worthington, an A-level student at Highfields. 'But in other ways, they are worlds apart.'

Indeed, Bemrose and Highfields are proving that schools don't have to find partners on the other side of the globe to offer students a glimpse of a different way of life. The link started in 2003, when a group of students from the two schools won a £20,000 Barclays New Futures award. The aim of their project was to bring together children from rural Derbyshire and inner-city Derby to promote a greater understanding of cultural differences. Since then, secondary students from Highfields and Bemrose have worked together to organize a series of joint events for children from their main primary feeder schools: everything from drama, dance and storytelling workshops to trips to Derby County's football ground.

Highfields serves a stable, rural community and inevitably there is an element of insularity. Not only does everyone here speak English, they speak it with the same vowel sounds. Alex Worthington was one of a group of students who decided that the next generation at Highfields should have the chance to experience a multi-ethnic environment.

In part the motivation was to promote tolerance and prevent prejudice, but also simply to widen the horizons of those brought up in the narrow society of the Derwent Valley. 'You don't learn about other cultures or religions from a textbook,' he says. 'You learn through being with people and getting to know them. You need to meet people from different backgrounds. Otherwise you're going to be in for a big shock when you leave school and go to university.'

Bemrose is certainly diverse. Not just because it serves a large Asian and Afro-Caribbean community and celebrates a range of religious festivals, but also because it has a relatively high turnover of students. 'You become very accepting of people,' says Bemrose's head of languages, Jackie James. 'It makes you outward-looking. New faces are no big deal.'

It was a surprise, then, for the Bemrose students to visit one of the Highfields feeder primaries, Darley Churchtown in Darley Dale, and see an entire classroom of white faces. 'I don't know who was more amazed, the children from Bemrose, or the children from Darley Dale,' says Ms James. 'When we walked through the door, we were met with wide-eyed amazement by some of the children. It was the first time most of them had seen a non-white face, other than on television.'

The children from Darley Dale had another surprise when they visited the Bemrose feeder primary Bishop Lonsdale, and found a new, spotlessly clean, state-of-the-art building, and not the run-down graffiti-clad sheds some of them had been expecting.

After several years of regular meetings, there are no more surprises and the children have become comfortable working together. The secondary students from Bemrose and Highfields are responsible for organizing the joint events; they handle everything from booking artists and venues to arranging catering. Inevitably it has meant spending a good deal of time at each other's schools and has given plenty of scope for reflection on the difference between life in the city and the country town.

Highfields is now drawing up plans to become a specialist performing arts college, and has named Bemrose as an official partner, despite the distance between the two. 'Lots of schools are making links with partner schools overseas,' says Alex Worthington. 'But it's also important to realise how much you can learn from schools closer to home.'

Chapter 23

Classroom pets

Animals can teach children about human behaviour and body language, about parenting skills and social responsibility. Learning to care for an animal is often their first step towards learning to care for others. But if you decide to keep a pet at school, how can you ensure it's well looked after? And is it a good idea at all?

Why get a classroom pet?

Death and babies are two of the most difficult subjects for teachers. Having an animal living its comparatively short life cycle in the classroom is a good way to explain to curious children some of life's big questions. But pets can also help in other ways. They teach children responsibility. So rather than pulling the wings off an insect, they have to try feeding, watering and warming it. The International Association of Human–Animal Interaction met in Rio de Janeiro, Brazil in 2001 to discuss the role animals could play in schools and came to the overwhelmingly positive conclusion that they 'encourage the moral, spiritual and personal development of each child'.

Regular contact with animals has also been shown to make children calmer, better able to concentrate and more co-operative in class. A study of 37 urban and rural elementary schools in Australia found that pets not only increased class cohesiveness but also generated a calm and orderly environment, modified disruptive behaviour and reduced friction.

Animals are also the secret weapon for Green Chimneys school in New York, which has been dealing successfully for more than 50 years with pupils from troubled backgrounds, most of whom have been involved in gang warfare and drug dealing. Each of its 300 pupils is assigned an animal, and while many of the children won't speak to therapists (many won't speak at all), they often form a bond with the animals – and then begin to talk to them. Once they've taken the plunge with a friendly pet, most then find it easier to move on and talk to their peers and the adults around them.

It is not only behaviour that can be improved, however. A 2002 study from the University of Warwick found that pets can make children healthier by stimulating the immune system. Children with pets at home were found to have more stable levels of antibodies and were recorded as being in school nine days a year more than those without pets. The effects were particularly marked in primary-aged children between 5 and 8 years old.

Before you take the plunge...

Just like getting a pet at home, the decision to bring an animal into the classroom should not be taken lightly. Just because you and your class can survive in a small, draughty temporary hut, it doesn't mean an animal can. The Royal Society for the Prevention of Cruelty to Animals (RSPCA) points out that a classroom can be a difficult environment for a pet, and encourages teachers to work their way through its stringent guidelines before making that visit to the pet shop.

Be clear about what the pet is for. Don't get an animal just to make yourself popular or because you know of a rabbit needing a good home. Getting a pet should be about sharing your love of animals and demonstrating responsible ownership. It's not fair to the animal to have half-hearted and reluctant care. It also sends out bad messages to a class if it sees an animal being neglected, or if pupils come to think of its care as a burden.

It can be easy to underestimate the costs of care, so it's always worth doing a few sums first. While most pets are likely to be cheap to buy, the cost of bowls, cages, bedding and food can add up. Vets' bills are rising by an average of 11 per cent a year and pet insurance starts at around £5 a month. These costs may not be in the school budget, and school fundraising may have other priorities – are you willing to foot the bills yourself?

And a pet will mean extra work. As the responsible adult, you will be in charge of feeding, cleaning and holiday care, as well as integrating it into lessons. You may well get help from keen pupils, but it's best to assume it'll all be up to you.

You've decided to get a pet – but what kind?

Ironically, animals best suited to humans – cats and dogs – are the least practical for the classroom. The best school pets are those that can be contained in cages, that can exercise themselves and that are happy to be left alone outside school hours.

Birds and rabbits are poor candidates because they tend to be sensitive to noise and lack of space. Rabbits are social animals and are best kept in groups: not very practical unless you have a particularly large and airy classroom. Reptiles need special conditions and careful handling. They are intolerant of temperature changes, have particular diets and can introduce salmonella bacteria into the classroom. And don't be tempted by the orphan fox cub someone has found by the roadside – keeping wildlife as pets is generally illegal.

Guinea pigs are one of the best choices – when they're properly socialized they enjoy being handled and rarely bite. They are also larger than gerbils, hamsters and mice, which can be more easily harmed by over-zealous handling. And they are awake during the day. Choosing nocturnal mammals, such as hamsters, will mean you miss most of the action, or they become unsettled and prone to biting because they are woken unnaturally.

For easy maintenance, try fish, worms or stick insects. They're also cheap and don't need much space. But worm watching can lack glamour – after the initial excitement of getting set up, children can find them dull and are unlikely to learn many of the facts of life from watching them.

Where do I get my pet?

Talk to local vets about good suppliers. Any pet brought into the classroom should come from a reputable dealer. This cannot be overemphasized. Animals can carry a host of parasites and diseases – those bought from dealers are usually bred in captivity and are subject to regular health checks. A good pet dealer will also be an important source of support and information for getting your pet settled in. And before buying your animal, make sure you handle it – if you need to don steel gloves, it's unlikely to enjoy the attentions of a class of curious children. Choosing the perfect pet is not just about finding the right species, but also about finding the right individual animal. Like all match-making, it can sometimes be a case of trial and error: a good dealer will usually allow you to have a trial run with a potential candidate at home for a few days. Even if you're sure you've found the perfect piranha for you, this can be a good idea, giving you a chance to get familiar with its behaviour before taking it into the classroom.

Is it hygienic to have a pet in the classroom?

Yes – as long as you follow basic rules for cleaning and husbandry, and make sure children wash their hands after handling. But there are other health issues to be aware of. Some animals, such as cats, birds, rabbits and small rodents – as well as the woodchip bedding often recommended for them – are highly allergenic. The number of people showing allergic symptoms to animals – sneezing, hives, skin reactions or breathing difficulties – is increasing, and you need to know how to cope with this kind of reaction. If an animal is housed in the classroom, it is your responsibility to ensure none of the pupils is allergic; this may mean organizing parental consent forms.

Although most of us are immune to diseases carried by domestic animals, any children with suppressed immune systems have an increased risk of infection. These include transplant patients, leukaemia or cancer patients, anyone who is HIV-positive and some people with asthma and skin conditions. In such cases, it's probably best to talk with parents and doctors. And all animals, no matter how tame, can bite, scratch or peck when handled. Have a plan for any injuries and teach children to be gentle.

What about weekends and holidays?

Some animals can be left over the weekend or for longer periods – fish, for example, can survive on special long-lasting food pellets. But most animals will need care, and the riskiest time for a pet is when it goes home with a family for the holidays. Injuries and deaths are common from neglect, or from jealous and undisciplined pets already with the family. If you don't take the pet home yourself, be certain that the family that does is committed and knows enough to give the right care. Comprehensive written guidelines for holiday arrangements should include advice on recognizing illness and agreement about who is responsible for costs, including vets' bills.

Mews or muse?

Once you've got your pet, you can make it sing for its supper. As well as providing general environmental education, pets can be used creatively in many curriculum areas. Science at key Stages 1 and 2 offers a range of opportunities for using your furry friend. Researching and interpreting data on the cost of keeping pets can form the basis of a maths project, and being able to watch an animal at close quarters stimulates creative work such as art, essays, poems and drama. A classroom pet can also be used as a metaphor for humans, allowing you to handle aspects of personal and social education – such as health, safety and behaviour – in an immediate and non-threatening way.

Using pets in the curriculum has been shown to be particularly effective with low-achievers and withdrawn children. There may be ancient reasons for this. The biophilia hypothesis formulated by Edward Wilson of Harvard University in 1984 – and still accepted – argues that we have an instinctive interest in animals. Wilson suggested that because early man needed to know as much as possible about animals to hunt effectively, so we are still programmed with an innate need to know about animal behaviour. Wilson's theory is that using animals to teach parts of the curriculum raises children's level of interest and triggers important learning techniques.

Stick insects are not enough

Some schools take the challenge of caring for animals extremely seriously. The Warriner school farm is a mixed 100-acre farm in Bloxham, north Oxfordshire, with a herd of Dexter cattle, ninety ewes, eight pigs, half a dozen anglo-nubian goats, chickens and working horses. This comprehensive also takes children: 11–16-year-olds from Banbury. The school sits alongside the farm – there is even an on-site classroom – so the children can spend a lot of time with the animals, and farm manager John Hirons teaches a 50 per cent timetable. Pupils help out at lunchtimes and after school, especially at busy times like lambing season. The farm went fully organic in 2001 and now teaches a range of issues around conservation and sustainability, as well as some of the basics – like where food comes from – and how farming contributes to the national economy. And there's a GCSE in rural science for those who want to prove they've mastered mucking out, ringing lambs' tails, milking cows and trimming cattle hooves.

What if I don't want a pet?

Children need to learn about animals, but the RSPCA points out that this is perfectly possible using soft toys, photographs and videos. Certainly books, magazines and videos can be a starting point as long as they give accurate information, and the internet offers everything from live web-cam footage of puppies playing to breeding details about mole rats. Asking children to bring pets from home for a pets' assembly or having a regular classroom visit from a trusted animal mascot are also simple ways of using pets that require no long-term planning or commitment.

The RSPCA suggests using field trips to parks, wildlife centres or local animal shelters as a humane alternative to having pets in the classroom, encouraging children to appreciate animals as part of a natural habitat. And the United Kingdom's network of wildlife trusts can offer advice on planting a butterfly garden or building a bird feed station. Or you can spend the money you might have put aside for a deluxe hamster wheel on adopting a manatee, Siberian tiger or blue whale. Many international animal protection organizations have adoption programmes for endangered species and in return for your sponsorship you get updated information, photographs and a resource pack. Or, if that seems too exotic, it's likely that your local animal shelter or wildlife centre will run a similar programme for more familiar native species or abandoned farm animals.

In practice

There's a homely feel about the behaviour and learning support block at Dronfield secondary school, near Sheffield. It's in what used to be the headteacher's house, which probably helps. So do the bright colours and comfortable Ikea furniture. But the relaxed domestic ambience is largely due to the presence of one Henry Fanshawe Smart.

He doesn't do much; mostly he just sprawls in front of the fireplace. Yet he is being credited with transforming pupils' attitudes, raising attendance rates and improving behaviour. Quite an achievement for a 6-month-old cavalier King Charles spaniel. So how does Henry do it? There's plenty of scientific evidence that looking after a pet can be therapeutic, and Wendy Brown, Dronfield's behaviour support manager, has much of it posted on the walls. 'He's a calming influence,' she explains. 'Children find it easier to talk about their problems if they're stroking Henry. And if someone is worked up about something I send them out to walk the dog, and they come back a different person.'

For children who have had a difficult weekend at home, it's a real tonic to be greeted on Monday morning by a four-legged friend. 'Henry offers unconditional love,' says Wendy. 'And, sadly, some of the children don't get that from their parents.' In return, the children are able to be affectionate towards the dog, without feeling self-conscious. 'It's not cool to show affection to your friends,' says Wendy, 'but it's fine to cuddle the dog.'

The chance to spend time with Henry is also an incentive for the children to keep up with their studies. If they don't finish their work, they don't get to see the dog. And he's more than just a pretty face. The school has developed an alternative curriculum for some of its students, using Henry as an educational resource. A 'skills for working life' qualification now includes an animal care element, and visiting speakers from the RSPCA explain about animal needs and responsible ownership.

Once the decision had been made to get a dog, the big question was, what sort? 'I was going to bring my own in,' says Wendy. 'But it's a West Highland terrier and it's just too crazy. The idea is to calm the kids down, not wind them up.' The school took advice from several sources before deciding on a cavalier King Charles: not too big, not too active, even-tempered – and unbearably cute.

Julie Smart, the school counsellor, takes him home with her at evenings and weekends. In return the dog bears her name – along with a tribute to the school's founder, Henry Fanshawe. At £450 apiece, pedigree spaniels don't come cheap, but Henry hasn't cost the school a penny. Two local charities put up the money to buy him, and a string of sponsors have been scrambling to make him the most pampered pooch in town. He's got a year's supply of food, £100 of toys, free veterinary care and a luxury portable kennel.

When 14-year-old Andrew comes into the room Henry rolls on to his back, ready to be made a fuss of. Andrew spends a lot of time in the student support area. He has attention deficit hyperactivity disorder, which requires medication, and a reputation for being difficult in class. Yet he is chatty and relaxed as he tickles Henry's pink belly. He talks about how important it is to look after animals properly, and tells me the student support block also has a pet rat, which he's taken home with him for a few days.

Wendy says that if Andrew's teachers could see him at this moment they would be astounded by the transformation. Even Andrew himself is aware of Henry's calming influence. 'Sometimes he comes and sleeps on my knee in the classroom,' he says. 'Then I can't fidget or I'd wake him up, so I just have to get on with my work.'

Chapter 24
Pupil power

Young people want a say in their education – and that's not just the lessons. It's the clothes they wear and the food they eat. They want their opinions to be heard, and more and more schools are listening. Pupil power is about democracy, equality and human rights. It's about children becoming key members of an educational partnership. It's also about vegetarian options in the canteen, new drinks machines and lockers for everyone. At its heart is that symbol of empowerment – the school council. Ridiculed when they first appeared back in the 1970s, councils are back in fashion. But does democracy make for better schools? How much power should pupils have? And are school councils really a vehicle for citizenship and change – or just an excuse to moan about the meals?

Why have a school council?

Because the days of children being seen and not heard have gone. Article 12 of the UN Convention on the Rights of the Child affirms 'the right of children to express their views on all matters of concern to them, and to have those views taken seriously in accordance with their age and maturity'. A school council is an effective way of allowing them to exercise that right. In December 2005, the Welsh Assembly made it a statutory requirement for all schools in Wales to establish a student council. Ofsted are also keen on pupil power: their inspection framework states that, where there is an established school council, inspectors must listen to its views and report back to it when the inspection is completed.

The benefits?

School councils help pupils develop important listening, mediating and problem-solving skills, and can make them feel valued and self-confident.

They can provide a link with the community, offer excellent public relations opportunities – and are also the perfect vehicle for learning about citizenship and stimulating an interest in politics. And, most importantly, there's growing evidence that pupil participation makes schools happier and more productive. A study conducted in 2002 by Derry Hannam, funded by the charity Community Service Volunteers, looked at 12 schools deemed 'more than usually student participative'. It found they had higher attendance rates and lower exclusion rates than would be expected. It also found that pupils had higher self-esteem and performed better academically than pupils in comparable but less participative schools.

Making a school council work

An effective student body has to be actively promoted and seen to be an integral part of what goes on in school. It should feature in prospectuses and newsletters, and have its own notice board. Agendas need to be publicized in advance so that people have the opportunity to contribute views, and minutes should be posted promptly in every classroom after meetings. Allowing council sessions to take place during lesson time instead of relegating them to the graveyard slot at the end of the day helps ensure a full turnout and sends a clear message about the value of the council. Having regular meetings – twice every half-term should be a minimum – also makes sure the council gets the chance to tackle up-to-the-minute concerns, and may help keep meetings short and purposeful. A time limit is a sensible precaution. Time also needs to be set aside for 'class councils' where school councillors can get a feel for grassroots opinion and feedback on the decisions that have been made.

Most schools find an adult facilitator makes meetings more productive. It's a key role; the person must resist the temptation to keep order or steer the councillors in the 'right' direction. Their job is to stimulate, encourage and recommend useful resources. Inviting a range of authority figures – the headteacher, the bursar, a governor – can give meetings a sense of importance as long as staff realize that they are there to answer to the council, not dictate to it.

Toilets and greasy chips

Most council discussions tackle apparently mundane matters. The three most common topics for discussion in secondary schools are facilities, meals and uniform. 'Playground issues' top the list in primary schools. Comparing the relative merits of hopscotch and basketball may seem humdrum, but what the council discusses is less important than the freedom to express opinions and make decisions. A sense of ownership can also transform attitudes and have a knock-on effect on behaviour, even if it's only over seemingly trivial issues. 'They picked the decor for the new toilets,' says Sarah Purtil of Kingsbury high school in the London borough of Brent. 'It's hideous. We wouldn't have chosen it in a million years. But it hasn't been graffitied or vandalized once.'

The Summerhill experience

Summerhill – an independent school founded in Suffolk in 1921 – is perhaps the best known 'democratic' school. Pupils decide whether or not to attend lessons, and at the centre of school life is a weekly democratic meeting at which all rules and punishments are decided. The opinion of a senior member of staff carries no more weight that that of the youngest pupil. 'We're trailblazers,' says headteacher Zoe Readhead. 'In recent years there's been a surge of interest in what we do here.' The school has official visiting days when pupils and staff from other schools can see Summerhill democracy in action, and although few take on the full-blown model, many are inspired to find new ways of getting pupil's voices heard.

There are a handful of similar schools around the world – almost all independents. But the Democratic School of Hadera in Israel is a state-run school that, like Summerhill, has optional lessons and an all-powerful student parliament. It also has a lengthy waiting list (entry is decided by drawing lots) and its popularity has led to the opening of other similar schools, all supported by the Israeli government and used as training schools for new teachers.

How much power should a council have?

At one extreme is the Summerhill model of one person, one vote – teachers and students alike. At the other are schools where the council is little more than a debating club and the head's word is always final. Most schools aim for something in between. At Wolverhampton grammar school, for example, head Bernard Trafford says that if the council voted to abolish school uniform, its views would be considered but not necessarily adopted. 'It wouldn't be their decision, but it wouldn't be my decision either. We would include governors and parents too. The council would be part of the decision-making process.'

The important thing is to ensure the council has credibility – perhaps by allowing it to spend money. If its opinions are routinely ignored, students will soon become cynical. You need to be prepared to act on council decisions even if you don't like them. Define some areas where the council can have autonomy – if necessary, agree a written constitution – but also be clear about areas in which it has no authority. If students understand the extent of their powers they are less likely to become disillusioned. Above all, be brave. If a council is nothing more than a focus group it will fail.

Won't there be chaos?

No. Few schools report councils acting irresponsibly. In fact, a common complaint is that councils tend to be too conservative: heads report councils giving them a hard time for not getting tough over drugs, or voting for more homework.

With this in mind, it may be worth encouraging an interesting mix of pupils to stand for election: a lively school council cannot be an elitist organization packed with the usual worthies. And make sure elected members canvass the opinions of everyone in their class, not just the voluble few. A councillor's job is to represent the people who elect them, not to argue their own views.

Being patient

Councils need to understand that they probably won't be able to make a difference overnight. One council was keen that every pupil should have a decent-sized locker in working order. Although the school accepted that the request was reasonable, it took four years to accomplish. Young people can expect instant results, whereas, as all staff know, schools change very slowly. It's important to get a balance between keeping things moving (and keeping morale high) and working through the proper processes for implementing decisions. Try to act quickly on those council decisions which are straightforward and where things need to take longer, agree a time-scale and provide regular progress updates.

Because the pace of change can be slow, it's important to ensure the council has continuity. It may be tempting to swap councillors every term, but allowing pupils to serve one-year stints – or even longer – will give them time to develop skills and bring projects to fruition. If you want to involve more pupils, set up several councils, each with its own responsibility for particular areas of school life.

'Mrs Jones is ugly, useless and horrible...'

Many schools forbid councils to discuss individual teachers. Others believe this is a fundamental part of the democratic process – after all, teachers discuss pupils at staff meetings. John Bangs, head of education at the NUT says allowing direct criticism of staff is unprofessional. 'It breeds fear and mistrust,' he says. 'That's never a healthy atmosphere.' But one head who does permit students to voice concerns about teaching methods claims that 'no one's ever been vindictive, and the criticisms have usually been valid and productive'. A possible compromise is to allow discussion about subjects and the way they are taught, but not about individual teachers.

If you do allow a council to criticize – or compliment – individual staff, make sure staff have the right to reply direct to the council. At one school where pupils complained about the attitude of the catering staff, the head of catering asked some of the council representatives to work in the kitchens one lunchtime to experience the pressure her staff were under. The matter was resolved with increased understanding on both sides.

'Well you chose her...'

Many schools now involve pupils at all stages of the staff appointments process – from drawing up a job description to giving feedback on sample lessons and conducting their own interviews. Student panels can be good at asking pertinent questions and skilled at reading body language.

Once pupils have helped to select teachers, they can contribute to their professional development by becoming involved in appraisals and feedback on schemes of work. In Austria – where the school council system extends to regional and national assemblies – children even help to plan lessons.

Can school councils work at primary level?

Research by the National Foundation for Educational Research in 2002 suggested that satisfaction with the school council tends to be higher in primary than in secondary schools. Primaries have a structure that makes councils work; children spend most of their days in form groups, so councillors have a closer connection with their constituency. And class councils can be a natural extension of circle time. Smaller numbers also make the process more manageable; in some small primaries it may even be possible to have 'whole-school' councils rather than elected representatives.

Beyond the council

The next logical step is to invite pupils to become an integral part of the school's decision-making process, rather than a separate body. Having pupil representatives at staff meetings, curriculum review meetings, even budget management meetings, helps students understand how schools work. And it needn't be a token gesture. Many schools find pupils bring a fresh perspective and make valuable contributions. It has been tried before. The 1977 Taylor report on governing bodies recommended pupil governors. Some authorities followed this up, but the Conservatives scrapped the plans before the end of the decade.

Structured meetings are just one way of giving students a voice. Other expressions of pupil power include peer support groups – where students offer each other counselling and advice – and student newspapers. Real pupil power is when all areas of school life – assemblies, plays, concerts, sports events – provide an opportunity not just to participate but to organize and take the initiative.

Towards democracy

A study commissioned in 2003 by the Association of Teachers and Lecturers concluded that school councils work best where democracy, participation and welfare are part of the school ethos. If you're not sure whether you work in an autocracy or democracy, look around. Are staff valued, consulted and free to voice opinions without fear of reprisal? Does the head operate an open-door policy? Are there clear grievance procedures for staff and pupils? Do pupils have the right to sit exams that the school believes they will fail? Are prefects elected by the pupils or chosen by the staff? Are comment boxes and questionnaires an accepted part of school life?

Headteachers who have tried to make their schools more democratic usually admit the process is hard work. Staff may feel vulnerable, parents may worry about discipline, pupils may become pushy and rude. The process of empowerment can be slow and painful. Staff and management will need to develop thick skins. 'But in the end it is worth it,' says Bernard Trafford. 'A democratic school is a happier place for everyone – and I've got the questionnaires to prove it.'

Resources

These resources are intended to help those wanting to explore further the issues raised in each chapter. They are by no means exhaustive, but they offer helpful lines of enquiry and reflect the things which I found useful during my own research.

First listed are organizations with expertise specific to each chapter. Typically, they can offer practical advice, and produce teaching resources and helpful publications. Wherever possible, web addresses have been included and these usually make the best first port of call. Suggestions for wider reading come next, both in traditional and on-line form.

1 The teaching voice

Voice Care Network UK
www.voicecare.org.uk
01926 864000

Berry, C., *Your Voice and How to Use It*, London: Virgin Books, 2000.
Linklater, K., *Freeing the Natural Voice*, Los Angeles: QSM, 1988.
Martin, S. and Darnley, L., *The Teaching Voice*, Chichester: Whurr, 2004.
Rodenburg, P., *The Right to Speak*, London: Methuen, 1992.

www.soundranger.com

2 Truancy

Blyth, E. and Milner, J. (Eds), *Improving School Attendance*, London: RoutledgeFalmer, 1999.
Reid, K., *Tackling Truancy in Schools: A Practical Manual for Primary and Secondary Schools*, London: RoutledgeFalmer, 1999.

Reid, K., *Truancy: Working with Teachers, Parents and Schools*, London: RoutledgeFalmer, 2002.

www.bromcom.com
www.dfes.gov.uk/schoolattendance
www.easytrace.co.uk
www.pearsonphoenix.com
www.sentinel-2000.com
www.truancycall.com

3 Nits

Community Hygiene Concern
www.nits.net
020 7686 4321

Brownlow, M., *I've Got Nits*, Wincanton: Ragged Bears, 2001.
Moss, M., *Scritch Scratch*, London: Orchard Books, 2002.
Sawyer, J. and MacPhee, R., *Head Lice to Dead Lice*, Eastbourne: New Leaf, 2001.

4 Bereavement

The Child Bereavement Trust (CBT)
www.childbereavement.org.uk
01494 446648

ChildLine
www.childline.org.uk
Helpline 0800 1111

Cruse Bereavement Care
www.crusebereavementcare.org.uk
020 8939 9530

Holland, J., *Coping with Bereavement: A Handbook for Teachers*, Cardiff: Cardiff Academic Press, 1996.
Killick, S. and Lindeman S., *Giving Sorrow Words*, London: Lucky Duck Publishing, 1999.
Ward, B., *Good Grief 1* and *Good Grief 2*, London: Jessica Kingsley Publishers, 1995.

5 Junk food

The Caroline Walker Trust
www.cwt.org.uk
01726 844107

The Food and Behaviour Research Group
www.fabresearch.org
0870 7565960

The Food Commission
www.foodcomm.org.uk
0207 837 2250

The Food Standards Agency
www.food.gov.uk

The Health Education Trust
www.healthedtrust.com
01789 773915

The Human Nutrition Research Centre
www.mrc-hnr.cam.ac.uk
01223 426356

The Soil Association
www.soilassociation.org
0117 314 5000

Sustain
www.sustainweb.org
www.grab5.com
0207 837 1228

Orrey, J., *The Dinner Lady*, London: Bantam Press, 2005.

6 Homophobia

Families and Friends of Lesbians and Gay men
www.fflag.org.uk
01454 852 418

fpa
www.fpa.org.uk
0845 310 1334

School's Out!
www.schools-out.org.uk
020 7635 0476

Stonewall
www.stonewall.org.uk
020 7881 9440

7 Self harm

ChildLine in Partnership with Schools (CHIPS)
www.childline.org.uk
020 7650 3230

The National Inquiry into Self Harm
www.selfharmuk.org
020 7828 6085

The National Self Harm Support Network
www.nshn.co.uk

nch
www.nch.org.uk
020 7704 7000

The Royal College of Psychiatrists
www.rcpsych.ac.uk
020 7235 2351

Young Minds
www.youngminds.org.uk
0800 018 2138

8 Teenage suicide

The Depression Alliance
www.depressionalliance.org
020 7278 6747

Mental Health Foundation
www.mentalhealth.org.uk

Mind
www.mind.org.uk

Papyrus
www.papyrus-uk.org
0870 170 4000

The Samaritans
www.samaritans.org
020 8355 1984

Trust for the Study of Adolescence
www.tsa.uk.com
01273 693311

9 When you're sick

Association of Teachers and Lecturers (ATL)
www.atl.org.uk
020 7930 6441

Benenden Healthcare
www.benenden-healthcare.org.uk
0870 7545 731

National Association of Schoolmasters Union of Women Teachers (NASUWT)
www.nasuwt.org.uk
0121 453 6150

National Union of Teachers (NUT)
www.nut.org.uk
0845 300 1669

Teacher Support Network (TSN)
www.teachersupport.org.uk
020 7554 5200

Cooper, M. *The Well Teacher*, Stafford: Network Educational Press, 2000.

10 Teachers' sabbaticals

The British Council organizes an extensive range of exchange and visit opportunities including the Fulbright Teacher Exchange.
www.britishcouncil.org
028 9024 8220 ext. 226

Farmington Institute for Christian Studies offers half or full term fellowships at a range of universities, open to primary and secondary teachers of RE.
www.farmington.ac.uk
01865 271965

The Goldsmiths' Company awards Goldsmiths' Mid-Career Refreshment Grants: awards of up to £5,000 for primary and secondary across the United Kingdom for travel, usually overseas, of four to six weeks. Applicants must have done at least ten years continuous service, but should be under the age of 55.
http://www.thegoldsmiths.co.uk/education/refreshgrant.htm
020 7606 7010

League for the Exchange of Commonwealth Teachers (LECT) organizes one year exchanges to Australia, Canada or New Zealand. UK-wide, but applicants must have been in the profession for three years or more.

www.lect.org.uk
0870 770 2636

The National College for School Leadership has opportunities for heads and deputies to pursue a research project, in teams or as individuals. Based on 30 days of flexible absence from school, with £5,000 awarded to meet cost of cover. Other bursaries also available.
www.ncsl.org.uk
0115 872 2040

Oxbridge colleges with well-established fellowship schemes include Newnham, Sidney Sussex and Corpus Christi (all Cambridge) and Corpus Christi, St Peter's and Merton (Oxford). In addition to the individual college programmes, Oxford also organises study visits for teachers in the summer holidays.
Cambridge admissions
01223 333308
Oxford admissions
01865 288000

Voluntary Service Overseas (VSO)
www.vso.org.uk

Winston Churchill Memorial Trust offers grants to cover an overseas stay of between four and eight weeks. Not exclusive to teachers, but applicants put forward travel proposals which must fall under the trust's nominated categories, one of which is usually connected to education.

www.wcmt.co.uk
020 7584 9315

11 Using questions

Anderson, L.W. and Kratchwohl, D.R., *Taxonomy of Learning, Teaching and Assessing: A Revision of Bloom's Taxonomy of Educational Objectives*, London: Addison Wesley, 2001.

Wragg, E.C. and Brown, G., *Questioning in the Primary School*, London: RoutledgeFalmer, 2001.

Wragg, E.C. and Brown, G., *Questioning in the Secondary School*, London: RoutledgeFalmer, 2001.

12 Handwriting

British Dyslexia Association
www.bda-dyslexia.org.uk

Dyspraxia Foundation
www.dyspraxiafoundation.org.uk

National Handwriting Association
www.nha-handwriting.org.uk

Sassoon, R., *Handwriting of the 20th Century*, London: RoutledgeFalmer, 1999.
Sassoon, R., *The Art and Science of Handwriting*, Bristol: Intellect, 2000.
Sassoon, R., *Handwriting: The Way to Teach it*, London: Paul Chapman, 2003.

13 Emotional intelligence

Antidote
www.antidote.org.uk
020 7247 3355

Centre for Applied Emotional Intelligence
www.emotionalintelligence.co.uk
01452 741106

National Emotional Literacy Interest Group
www.nelig.com

The School of Emotional Literacy
www.schoolofemotional-literacy.com
01452 741106

Gardner, H., *Frames of Mind: Theory of Multiple Intelligences*, London: Fontana Press, 1993.
Goleman, D., *Emotional Intelligence: Why It Can Matter More Than IQ*, London: Bloomsbury, 1996.
Goleman, D., *Working with Emotional Intelligence*, London: Bloomsbury, 1999.
Park, J., Haddon, A. and Goodman, H., *The Emotional Literacy Handbook*, London: David Fulton, 2003.
Sharp, P., *Nurturing Emotional Literacy: A Practical Guide for Teachers, Parents and Those in the Caring Professions*, London: David Fulton, 2001.

14 Thinking skills

Society for the Advancement of Philosophical Enquiry and Reflection in Education
www.sapere.net

The University of the First Age
www.ufa.org.uk
0121 202 2347

Claxton, G., *Building Learning Power: Helping Young People Become Better Learners*, Bristol: TLO, 2002.
Fisher, R., *Stories for Thinking*, Oxford: Nash Pollock, 1996.
Fisher, R., *Teaching Children to Think*, Cheltenham: Nelson Thornes, 2005.
Wallace, B. (Ed.), *Teaching Thinking Skills across the Primary Curriculum*, London: David Fulton, 2002.

www.braingym.org
www.case-network.org
www.edwdebono.com
www.mind-map.com
www.optimal-learning.net

15 Personalized learning

Connetix
www.connetix.co.uk

Adcock, J., *Teaching Tomorrow: Personal Tuition as an Alternative to School*, Nottingham: Education Now, 2003.
Meighan, R., *Flexischooling: Education for Tomorrow, Starting Yesterday*, Nottingham: Education Now, 1988.
Meighan, R., *John Holt: Personalised Learning Instead of Uninvited Teaching*, Nottingham: Educational Heretics Press, 2002.
Smith, A., Lovatt, M. and Wise, D., *Accelerated Learning: A User's Guide*, Stafford: Network Educational Press, 2003.

16 Teaching children to read

The Book Trust
www.booktrust.org.uk
020 8516 2977

The Child Literacy Centre
www.childliteracy.com

The National Literacy Trust
www.literacytrust.org.uk
020 7828 2435

The Reading Reform Foundation
www.rrf.org.uk

Cullingford, C. *How Children Learn to Read and How to Help Them*, London: RoutledgeFalmer, 2001.
Duncan, H. and Parkhouse, S., *Improving Literacy Skills for Children with Special Educational Needs*, London: RoutledgeFalmer, 2000.
Geekie, P., Cambourne, B. and Fitzsimmons, P., *Understanding Literacy Development*, Stoke on Trent: Trentham Books, 1999.
Morrow, L.M., *Literacy Development in the Early Years: Helping Children Read and Write*, London: Allyn and Bacon, 1993.
Nutbrown, C., *Recognising Early Literacy Development*, London: Paul Chapman, 1997.

www.standards.dfes.gov.uk/literacy

17 Promoting creativity

CAPEUK
www.capeuk.org
0113 200 7035

Creative Partnerships
www.creative-partnerships.com

National Campaign for the Arts
www.artscampaign.org.uk
020 7333 0375

Craft, A., *Teaching Creativity: Principles and Practice*, London: RoutledgeFalmer, 1999.
Craft, A., Jeffrey, B. and Leibling, M., *Creativity in Education*, London: Continuum, 2001.
Cropley, A.J., *Creativity in Education and Learning: A Guide for Teachers and Educators*, London: RoutledgeFalmer, 2001.
Hargreaves, A., *Teaching in the Knowledge Society: Education in the Age of Insecurity*, Maidenhead: Open University Press, 2003.
Jeffrey, B. and Woods, P., *The Creative School: A Framework for Success, Quality and Effectiveness*, London: RoutledgeFalmer, 2003.
Robinson, K., *Out Of Our Minds: Learning to be Creative*, Oxford: Capstone Publishing, 2001.

18 Going green

Council for Environmental Education
www.cee.org.uk
0118 950 2550

Encams
www.encams.org
01942 824620

Global Action Plan
www.globalactionplan.org.uk
020 7405 5633

Sustrans
www.sustrans.org.uk
0845 113 0065

19 Using volunteers

Governornet
www.governornet.co.uk
08000 722 181

Information for School and College Governors
www.governors.fsnet.co.uk
020 7229 0200

National Association of Governors and Managers
www.nagm.org.uk
0121 643 5787

National Governors' Council
www.ngc.org.uk
0121 616 5104

School Governors One Stop Shop
www.schoolgovernors-oss.co.uk
0870 241 3883

Creese, M. and Earley, P., *Improving Schools and Governing Bodies*, London: RoutledgeFalmer, 1999.
Dean, J., *The Effective School Governor*, London: RoutledgeFalmer, 2000.
Marriott, D., *The Effective School Governor*, Stafford: Network Education Press, 1998.
Sallis, J., *Basics for School Governors*, Stafford: Network Educational Press, 2000.
Wragg, T. and Partington J.A., *Handbook for School Governors*, London: RoutledgeFalmer, 1995.

20 Artists in residence

Arts Council
www.artscouncil.org.uk
0845 300 6200

Arts Council Wales
www.artswales.org.uk
029 20 376500

Scottish Arts Council
www.scottisharts.org.uk
0131 226 6050

Writing Together
www.booktrust.org/writingtogether
020 8516 2976

Coe, M. and Sprackland, J., *Our Thoughts Are Bees: Writers Working with Schools*, London: Wordplay Press, 2005.

21 The learning environment

Building Schools for the Future
www.bsf.gov.uk
01325 391716

Council for Architecture and the Built Environment (CABE)
www.cabe-education.org.uk
020 7960 2400

Design Council
www.designcouncil.org.uk
020 7420 5200

Partnerships for Schools
www.p4s.org.uk
020 7273 0001

School Works
www.school-works.org
0845 456 1803

22 School links

British Council
www.britishcouncil.org
020 7389 4359 (England and Wales),
0131 447 8024 (Scotland) or
028 9024 8220 (Northern Ireland)

Link Community Development
www.lcd.org.uk
020 7691 1818

Times Educational Supplement
www.tes.co.uk/make_the_link

UK One World Linking Association
www.ukowla.org.uk
01672 861001

23 Classroom pets

Farms for City Children
www.farmsforcitychildren.co.uk
01837 810785

National Association of Farms for Schools
www.farmsforschools.org.uk
01422 882708

RSPCA
www.rspca.org.uk
0870 333 5999

Society for Companion Animal Studies (SCAS)
www.scas.org.uk
www.nationalpetweek.org.uk
01877 330996

www.petwebsite.com

24 Pupil power

Children's Rights Alliance for England
www.crights.org.uk
020 7278 8222

The Organising Bureau of European School Student Unions
www.obessu.org

School Councils UK
www.schoolcouncils.org
020 8349 1917

Summerhill School
www.summerhillschool.co.uk

Baginsky, M. and Hannam, D., *School Councils: the Views of Students and Teachers*, available from the NSPCC.
Inman, S. and Burke, H., *School Councils: An Apprenticeship in Democracy*, available from the Association of Teachers and Lecturers.
Osler, A. (Ed.), *Citizenship and Democracy in Schools: Diversity, Identity, Equality*, Stoke on Trent: Trentham Books, 2000.
Trafford, B., *Participation, Power-sharing and School Improvement*, Nottingham: Educational Heretics Press, 1998.

Index

Amos effect: and truancy 13
artists in residence: benefits of 126–127, 128; costs of 127; support for 130
Arts Council, the 127, 128, 129, 130
Association of Teachers and Lecturers (ATL), the 158
attendance: improving pupil 13–15

Bereavement: in children 21–22; effects of 25–26; school policy on 25; support 24
Brain Bank Connectivity 104
Breathing 4, 5
British Council, the 139, 141, 142
buddy schemes 50, 85, 158
bug-busting 18, 20
Building Schools for the Future 132
bullying 19; homophobic 36–37, 39; management 39; and self harm 41; and suicide 47

Centre for Suicide Research 42
Child Bereavement Trust 24
ChildLine 26, 40
Classrooms of the Future 132
Cognitive Acceleration through Science Education (CASE) 87
Commission for Architecture and the Built Environment (CABE) 137
Community Service Volunteers 154
Consumers' Association, the 31

Creative Partnerships 128, 130
creativity: definition of 101–102; employment and 102–103; national curriculum and 103–104; teaching and 102, 103, 105

death 21, 22
Department for Education and Skills (DfES) 10, 52, 68, 77, 82, 83, 91, 117, 121, 128, 132
Department of Transport 109
design: results and 135; schools and 113–114, 132–137
Design Council, the 132, 133, 137
Development Education Association, the 142
diabetes 30

Eco-Schools 110, 111
Education for All 39
Education for Sustainable Development 114
emotional intelligence: definitions of 82; history of 81; importance of 83; introducing 85; IQ and 84–85
Employment Equality (Sexual Orientation) Regulation 35
Encams 110, 112
energy consumption, schools and 110–111
exchange programmes 59–60

Food and Behaviour Research Group 29, 31

Gardner, Howard 84, 101
Global Action Plan 111
Goldsmiths' Company: grants from 61, 62–64
governors 120–112

handwriting: exams and 77; history of 73; pens and 75–76; types of 74–75
head lice: history of 17–18; treating 18–20
Heads, Teachers and Industry (HTI) 61
health 1, 17–20, 52–57
health insurance 55
Healthy Schools 38, 43
homophobia: incidence of 36; tackling 38–40
homophobic language 37
Human Nutrition Research Centre 29

immune system 22
in practice: artists in residence 130–131; creativity 105–106; going green 115–116; handwriting 79–80; healthy eating 32–34; pets 151–152; sabbaticals 62–64; school links 143–145; voice 8–9
International Obesity Task Force 30

Japan 21 143
junk food: definition of 28; effects on children 29–30; and mental health 30–31

learner: types of 91
learning styles: types of 90–91
Link Community Development 139, 142
linking: funding for 141; schools and 138–145; support for 142
litter 112–113, 115–116

mental health: nutrition and 30
mind-mapping 89
mourning rituals 22
multiple intelligences 84, 101

National Association of Governors and Managers 121
National Association of Head Teachers (NAHT) 53
National Association of Parent Teacher Associations 121–122
National Association of Schoolmasters Union of Women Teachers (NASUWT) 39, 118
National Centre for Volunteering 117, 122
National Diet and Nutrition Survey 28
National Inquiry into Self Harm 40–41, 45
National Self-Harm Network 41
National Union of Teachers (NUT) 55, 157
nch (National Children's Home) 41

obesity 30
occupational health nurses 56
Oxford and Cambridge Schoolteacher fellowships 61–62

parents: handwriting and 78; nits and 20; self harm and 44; truancy and 12–13; volunteering and 118–119
peer mentors 50, 85, 158
personalized learning: definition of 90–91; teaching and 91–92; technology and 92–93
pets: choosing 147–148; curriculum and 149–150
posture: voice and 4, 5

questions: higher-order 68–69; lower-order\factual recall 68–69; using 69–72

recycling 111–112
Romans 18
Royal Society for the Prevention of Cruelty to Animals (RSPCA) 147, 150–151

sabbaticals: entitlement to 58
Samaritans, the 42, 48–49, 51
school councils 153–159
school policy: bereavement 25; handwriting 78–79; homophobia 35; suicide prevention 50–51; volunteers 118
school run 109
school travel adviser 110
Section 28; repeal of 35
self-esteem 19, 23, 41, 44, 47, 78, 81, 105, 154
self harm: causes of 41–42; incidence of 40–41; response to 43–45
sickness: incidence of 52
Six Hats 89
Social Issues Research Centre 31
software systems: and personalized learning 93; and truancy 15
Soil Association, the 28, 33
staff rooms 136–137
Stonewall 36, 39
stress 53–54
suicide: dealing with 48–49; 'epidemics' of 50; factors in 48; self harm and 47; teenagers and 46–47, 50
Summerhill School 155
supply: costs of 52
Sustrans 109–110

Teacher Support Network 56, 136
teaching exchange 59–60
thinking skills: children and 87; definition of 86, 88, 89; teaching of 87
truancy: crime and 11; numbers of 10–11; recording 10, 11, 15
Trust for the Study of Adolescence 47, 51

UK One World Linking Association (UKOWLA), the 139

voice: environment and 6; journal of 3; use of 7
Voice Care Network UK 7
voice clinics 3
Voluntary Service Overseas (VSO) 60, 142
volunteers: legal obligations and 117; sourcing 119–120; training of 123; use of 118, 122

water: saving 111–112
water consumption 111–112
wind power 111

zinc: deficiency of, and behaviour 31

For Product Safety Concerns and Information please contact our EU representative GPSR@taylorandfrancis.com
Taylor & Francis Verlag GmbH, Kaufingerstraße 24, 80331 München, Germany

www.ingramcontent.com/pod-product-compliance
Lightning Source LLC
Chambersburg PA
CBHW051525230426
43668CB00012B/1747